Louis E. Lomax

TO A KILL BLACK MAN

An Original Holloway House Edition
HOLLOWAY HOUSE PUBLISHING CO.
LOS ANGELES, CALIFORNIA

*To Billy and Robin
from Dad,
in the faith that
you will build
a better world*

Published by
HOLLOWAY HOUSE PUBLISHING COMPANY
8060 Melrose Avenue, Los Angeles, CA 90046
All rights reserved. No part of this book may be reproduced or transmitted in any form or by any means, electronic or mechanical, including photocopying, recording or by any information storage and retrieval system, without permission in writing from the Publisher. Copyright © 1968, 1987 by Holloway House Publishing Company.
Any similarity to persons living or dead is purely coincidental.
International Standard Book Number 0-87067-731-4
Printed in the United States of America
Cover photograph by Jeffrey
Cover design by Claudia Warner

by Louis E. Lomax

FOREWORD

Much has happened to American society (and to World society, for that matter) in the twenty years since Louis E. Lomax wrote *To Kill A Black Man,* his highly acclaimed dual biography of Malcolm X and Martin Luther King, Jr.

Many of the Southern States are now home to the most integrated school systems in the country. Birmingham, Alabama, the site of so much tragedy during the Civil Rights era, has a black mayor, as do many cities, large and small, throughout the South. Many blacks, and especially educated, middle-class blacks, are returning to the South that they were taken from as children, or that their parents and grandparents left in the 1930s, 40s and 50s.

It has not become a perfect society, this new America. Far from it. But it is different than the America that Malcolm and Martin knew. It is now a country where a liberal black Democrat, Mike Espy, can get elected to Congress by unseating white conservative Republican Webb Franklin and become Mississippi's first black representative in Washington since the days of Reconstruction. That, in 1968, was nearly unthinkable.

They, Malcolm X, Martin Luther King, Jr., and yes, Louis E. Lomax who was close to both, would find it hard to believe today's America . . . an America they helped shape.

Lomax gained national prominence with such books as

To Kill A Black Man, The Black Revolt and *When the Word Is Given, The Reluctant African* and *Thailand: The War That Is, The War That Will Be.* He was very proud of all his work but particularly satisfied with *To Kill A Black Man,* the book about the two black leaders who had become his friends.

In his biography of both men, Lomax included material that Malcolm X did not tell in his autobiography; he dissects Malcolm's famous letters. Lomax wrote with the sympathy and understanding of a friend but was also quick to point out the shortcomings of both Malcolm X and Martin Luther King, Jr. and the reasons—as he saw it—they failed to achieve their goals and obtain the full support of the people.

To Kill A Black Man was published in late 1968. A few months later Louis E. Lomax left his job as a television commentator in California and moved his family to Baldwin, New York, where he became a lecturer at Hofstra University. He was killed in an automobile accident near Santa Rosa, New Mexico, on August 1, 1970 while returning home from a California lecture tour.

The text of this edition of *To Kill A Black Man* exactly follows the original. Following Lomax's text, on page 256, we have added a short epilogue.

The Editors

ACKNOWLEDGEMENTS

Although this book contains materials and information never published before, my primary task has been that of preparing a comparative analysis of two historic lives. The full details of lives led by men such as Malcolm X and Martin Luther King, Jr. are seldom, if ever, recorded; for these evangelists touched too many lives, influenced too many events for any one chronicler to inscribe the total account. But I hasten to express my thanks, and acknowledgements, to several writers and scholars whose works have been of invaluable aid to me as I prepared this volume.

Alex Haley's classic *Autobiography of Malcolm X* is, without doubt, the best biographical account ever written by an American black man.

George Breitman's collection of Malcolm's speeches under the title *Malcolm X Speaks* was not valuable to my research but it is the best prime source of Malcolm's ideas since my *When The Word Is Given* was published in 1963.

The same George Breitman has published *The Last Year Of Malcolm X*. Despite its unabashed socialist leanings I found this work to be a most fascinating attempt by a Marxist dialectician to fathom the mind of this century's most complex black man.

Martin Luther King's three books, *Where Do We Go From Here*, *Stride Toward Freedom* and *Why We Can't Quit*, are by far the best sources for those who wish to know more about his ideas. Biographically speaking, I found Lerone Bennett, Jr.'s *What Manner of Man* to be the most complete account of the nonviolent man from Georgia.

I owe a special debt to my wife, Robinette, for not only typing this manuscript but providing valuable criticism as well. Most of all I thank her for the companionship and lonely understanding every writer demands of those who love him.

But the real debt is to Malcolm X and Martin Luther King, Jr. They lived the courageous and troubled lives I seek here to interpret. Their legacy may yet change the world, particularly the United States.

INTRODUCTION

Two American black men—one an apostle of integration and nonviolence, the other a dynamic disciple of racial separatism—have trod the sacrificial road to classic martyrdom. Both men came from deeply religious backgrounds, the Negro Baptist church; both men sat in the pews as their fathers preached, both men went on to enrapture hundreds of thousands as they themselves preached. Both men deeply disturbed the American Establishment, both men caused irreparable divisions among the very people they dedicated their lives to reclaim. And toward the end of their lives they both led diminishing crowds as gathering clouds of public doubt formed over their heads, doubt about the essential correctness of the goals they had named and the methods they employed. Both men died from assassin's bullets as they stood in places they had been warned not to go; both had replied that they were ready to die if death was the price, the only price, they must pay for what they believed and were almost pathologically determined to accomplish. They were so much alike, these two black martyrs, yet no two men could have been more disparate. And their dissimilarities were epitomized by the nature of their deaths. One of them, Malcolm X, died at the hands of black men he loved and labored to save; the other, Martin Luther King, Jr., died at the hands of a white man whom Dr. King nonviolently embraced despite Malcolm's warnings that white men are amoral, endemic serpents and beasts.

These two assassinations are more, much more

than the elevation of two black men to martyrdom through violence; they lay bare the essential issues and practices that have rent the republic asunder. By examining the lives of these men, their doctrines and deaths, we have a classic framework in which to examine the issues of "integration versus separation," "violence versus nonviolence," "the relevance of the Christian ethic to modern life," and the question "can American institutions as now constructed activate the self-corrective power that is the basic prerequisite for racial harmony?"

I knew both Malcolm X and Martin Luther King well. I respected them both, and was a friend to both. In earlier writings, as will be true in this book, I was both approving and critical of certain aspects of their work. I cringed at Malcolm's over anti-white-ism and I never felt that King's effusive, though eloquent, proffering of love was a correct assessment of reality in an America contorted by a tradition of hate, in an America where as Stokely Carmichael so accurately phrased it, violence is as endemic as apple pie.

It is not too early to say that both men brought about tremendous changes in the American way of life; because they were here, this nation will never be the same. Death by assassination has elevated them to martyrdom in the eyes of different people who, without doubt, extol different philosophies and hope to execute dissimilar social miracles. Both died at the time of traumatic changes in their own public lives; Malcolm was edging away from his anti-whiteness in search of an accommodation with the ideas of Martin Luther King; and King announced that "Black is beautiful" as he sought an accommodation with the ~nated black masses of the nation. The social critic ~ut theorize that had both men lived longer they possibly would have traversed one hundred and eighty degrees to become as one.

In death, now, they are one; either they are one in the nothingness that is nonlife or they are one in the common immortality of men who struggle and die for a cause. Privately both Martin Luther King and Malcolm X were burdened men; they had little time or energy for themselves or their families. The world and its problems were forever in their living rooms and the anguished cry of the American black men pierced even their most intimate quiet. Malcolm will be shocked, but Martin will not, if somehow now they are together and they both sing:

> "Free at last,
> Free at last,
> Thank God Almighty,
> Free at last!"

> Louis E. Lomax
> Beverly Hills, California
> April 9, 1968

ONE

SOCIAL FORCES THAT
ROCKED THE CRADLES

It was night. The pregnant Negro woman, born of a West Indian mother and a white father, gathered her three children into her bedroom and then trembled with fright as hooded members of the Ku Klux Klan galloped around her Omaha, Nebraska, home screaming a demand that her husband, Earl Little, come out—perhaps to be killed. Although Louise Little was frightened the experience was not a new one. The Reverend Earl Little was a Baptist minister whose gospel was a mixture of Christianity and Garveyism, the notion that the American black man would never find peace in America and, thus, should return to Africa. Whereas white people fully supported black ministers who taught Jesus to Negroes they were both incensed at and frightened by any Negro who took to the pulpit to discuss white racism. Earl Little had been chased from town to town, from odd job to job, by white vigilante groups opposed to his preachings. Now the Klan had surrounded the Littles' Omaha home.

Mrs. Little had no alternative; she went to the front door, opened it, and then stood fully in the light of the moon for her tormentors to see that she was with child. Then she explained to them that her husband was not at home, that he was away on a preaching mission in Milwaukee. Louise Little returned to her children but the Klansmen did not immediately leave the house. Instead they continued to gallop around the home while screaming the dogma of white supremacy and smashing windows with their guns until every pane was in fragments. Then, their torches burning high, the Klansmen rode off into the night from whence they had come.

Earl Little contorted with anger and despair when he returned home to hear and see what had happened. A black man in that situation, at that time, had but one defense—flight. But Earl Little elected not to pack up and move to yet another town, to yet another odd job, until his wife gave birth.

The period of waiting was a time of reflection for Earl Little. The violence and family disruption that menaced him was merely a continuation of the pattern that had plagued him and his family for years. Little was born in Reynolds, Georgia; he had six brothers. Three of his brothers were killed by white men; one of them was lynched. Every probability was that the same fate awaited Earl Little, particularly if he remained in Omaha. Then, on May 19, 1925, the child was born. They named him Malcolm Little; he was successively to be known as "Big Red," "Malcolm X," and finally "El-Hajj Malik El-Shabazz."

The Little family moved to Milwaukee for a brief period, but Earl's search for economic independence from the white man caused him to move to Lansing, Michigan, where he bought a home and planned to open a grocery store. However it was just a matter of months before Little was in trouble with the white establishment of Lansing. As Malcolm later recalled it, his father had committed the sins of "wanting to own a store, living outside the

Negro district, and spreading unrest (Garveyism) among the 'good Niggers' of the town." Once again white violence lashed out at the Little family. In his astonishingly frank and brilliant autobiography, Malcolm X described the event in these moving terms:

"This time, the get-out-of-town threats came from a local hate society called the Black Legion. They wore black robes instead of white. Soon nearly everywhere my father went, Black Legionnaires were reviling him as an 'uppity nigger' for wanting to own a store, for living outside the Lansing Negro district, for spreading unrest and dissension among 'the good niggers.'

"As in Omaha, my mother was pregnant again, this time with my youngest sister. Shortly after Yvonne was born came the nightmare night in 1929, my earliest vivid memory. I remember being suddenly snatched awake into a frightening confusion of pistol shots and shouting and smoke and flames. My father had shouted and shot at the two white men who had set the fire and were running away. Our home was burning down around us. We were lunging and bumping and tumbling over each other trying to escape. My mother, with the baby in her arms, just made it into the yard before the house crashed in, showering sparks. I remember we were outside in the night in our underwear, crying and yelling our heads off. The white police and firemen came and stood around watching as the house burned down to the ground."

It was in that same year, 1929, that another American black child was born. Far from the bleak economic insecurity and social despair that engulfed the Little household, this birth was accomplished in the fabric of the Southern Negro middle class. The mother, born Alberta Williams, was herself the daughter of a successful Negro clergyman and had been educated at elite Negro secondary schools and colleges. The Williams family had shielded her from much of the raw bluntness of Southern segregation. The father, Martin Luther King, was a stark contrast. Born the son of a sharecropper, Martin King knew and lived segregation firsthand before he became the polished and accomplished clergyman who shepherded the four thousand members of Atlanta's Ebenezer Baptist Church. Despite his college training at Morehouse, Reverend King was the kind of man who enjoyed describing himself as having been trained at the "University of Hard Knocks." The hope of the family was that their first born, like Christ, would arrive on Christmas. The birth occurred two weeks later and they named the child Martin Luther King, Jr.

Despite the differences in their ages, birthplaces and environments, the social forces that rocked their cradles were already beginning the merciless chiseling that shapes men for martyrdom.

By 1930, the Little family was falling apart, caught in the wave of explosions of brutality that seize most Negro husbands who find themselves emasculated by white society. The children stood in horror as Reverend Little beat his wife; Malcolm was later to speculate that his father's brutality was a direct concomitant of his envy of Mrs. Little's education. It is not known just where Malcolm's mother received her schooling but, as Malcolm phrased it, "an educated woman cannot resist the temptation to correct an uneducated man. Every now and then, when she put those smooth words on him, he would grab her." In an even more trench-

ant analysis of the debilitating psychology that afflicted black male minds of that era, Malcolm goes
on to suggest that he was his father's favorite child
because he, Malcolm, was the lightest child. "I actually believe," Malcolm said, "that an anti-white
as my father was, he was so subconsciously afflicted
with the white man's brainwashing of Negroes that
he inclined to favor the light ones."

One feels that nonparallel father-son warmth as
Malcolm tells of his journeys with his clergyman-
father. Reverend Little is preaching his favorite
Christian sermon, *"That Little Black Train Is A-
comin',"* and the congregation shouts out praises
to the Lord as they are exhorted to "Git on board,
little children, git on board." And this gospel of
Christian promise carries allusions to the "Black
Train Homeward"—a popular slogan of Garveyism.
The implication that all black men should indeed
get on board was unmistakable. It was also through
his father that Malcolm made contact with the middle class Negroes of Lansing. Although they were
porters, bootblacks, chaffers, waiters and gamblers,
Malcolm had nothing but scorn for them. He indicted them for not wishing to return to Africa and
for being "Uncle Tom voices of the black race."
Instead, Malcolm cast his lot with the black masses
who were on W.P.A. or welfare. It is impossible
to read Malcolm without realizing that there was
beginning in him a class consciousness that was
to deeply shape his thinking and circumscribe his
death.

Then there is the phenomenon of Malcolm's
mother. In Malcolm's mind, and that is all that
really matters, she was so burdened by the white
blood in her veins that she favored her black
children and slighted her "light" child, Malcolm. She

whipped Malcolm; the father would not. Cultural sociologists will find interest in the fact that Malcolm's mother, for unexplained reasons, refused to eat pork and certain other foods including rabbit. Malcolm's father loved this "soul food" and the family diet became a source of deep husband and wife conflict. In later life Malcolm was to become unbearably outspoken against people, particularly Negroes, who ate pork.

If Malcolm's early youth, then, was being lived out in an open arena of family fights and personal insecurity, Martin Luther King, Jr. was taking his first steps in the cocoon fashioned by the black middle class value system. Love flowed like the mighty rivers of justice King was later to preach about, not only from his parents but from the members of the congregation who looked upon the young Martin as "our child" and showered him with affection and gifts. Although the black masses formed the majority of the membership of Ebenezer Baptist Church the social world of the Kings was that of the Negro middle class, the professionals. Young Martin grew up, as I did, in a black Georgia world peopled by ministers, doctors, and school teachers. Everybody preached against such things as adultery and stealing, but the one venial sin was ignorance. The education proffered us was of a poor quality, but this was more than overshadowed by the all but unbearable pressure that forced us to do our studies or be literally thrashed into insensibility. Negro history was pounded into our heads, at school and in the church, as well as in the home. We grew up in a society obsessed with a messiah complex, in the search and wait for a "Black Moses" who would deliver the Negro from the bondage of the white Egyptians by causing the waters to part in the Red Sea—later to be called "integration." But the raw reality of white racism was always there for us just as it was for Malcolm.

Martin recalls riding with his father one day as the Reverend King, Sr. drove through a stop sign. A white policeman pulled up and said:

"All right, boy, let me see your driver's license."

"I'm no boy," King senior shot back. And then he pointed to Martin. "This is a boy. I am a man, and until you call me one, I will not listen to you."

There was also a scene in an Atlanta shoe store:

"I will be happy to serve you if you just move to those seats in the rear," the white clerk said to Martin and his father.

"There is nothing wrong with these seats," King, Sr. replied. "We are quite comfortable here."

"Sorry," the clerk replied, "but you will have to move."

"We'll either buy shoes here," King, Sr. continued, "or we won't buy shoes at all." With this the father took young Martin by the hand and walked out of the store. And once they reached the sidewalk the elder King said, "I don't care how long I have to live with this system, I will never accept it."

No one who knew the elder King was surprised at these two episodes. Long before Martin was born (and how prophetic this was to be) he had refused to ride city busses after witnessing a brutal attack on Negro passengers. King, Sr. led the fight against segregated elevators in the Fulton County (Atlanta) court house, and was chairman of the committee that forced the city of Atlanta to bring salaries of Negro teachers into a parity with that paid to whites. The miracle, as Martin himself describes it, is that King, Sr. was never physically attacked by white vigilantes.

But somebody, almost certainly the white vigilantes, did strike violently in Lansing, Michigan, late in 1931. Earl Little turned up dead, half of his skull smashed in. The crime was never solved but the total conviction among blacks is that the klan beat Malcolm's father unconscious and then placed him on a streetcar track where the car all but cut his body in half. And with his funeral there began a six year effort to reinforce the glue that held the Little family together. But, as is so typical of the besieged mass black American family, there was no social alchemist who could have wrought this wonder.

First there was poverty. With the murder of Earl Little the family became so hungry that, in Malcolm's words, they could eat the holes from donuts. The sisters and brothers tried to keep things going by resorting to odd jobs. It did not work; there was no alternative to welfare. Malcolm sings with eloquent anguish as he remembers how much he hated welfare, how demeaned he was that he and his were forced to eat free flour and fatback, the largess of those who despised them and had murdered the breadwinner of the Little family.

Then there was the other man, Mrs. Little's new lover. Malcolm remembered the man's name but refused to mention it. Rather he writes that the man was big, black and mean. The Little children watch and listen as the big, black and mean man and their mother sleep together with no marriage plans. The mother desires marriage but the man is afraid of the responsibilities involved. There are too many children, too many mouths to feed, too many feet to be shod. And the white welfare man comes snooping around making certain that the black poor purchase their welfare food at the price of middle class sex habits. After a year the big, black, mean man left and never returned. Mrs. Little's mind began to tremble; she held long and protracted conversations with herself. Malcolm was caught stealing. The welfare department moved to place the Little children in "Christian homes" where they would receive a proper upbringing. By 1937, the Little family had been destroyed. The children were scattered among different homes in Lansing and they gathered together when they could to remember both the bitter and the sweet days. Mrs. Little was committed to a mental institution. Malcolm himself rendered the final judgement. "I truly believe that if ever a state social agency destroyed a family, it destroyed ours."

That was the year Martin Luther King, Jr. turned eight years old. He was in the third grade and even more advanced in Sunday School, in the teachings of Christ and the ethics of love and nonviolence. But young Martin had undergone a soul searching experience. He described it this way:

"For three or four years my inseparable playmates had been two white boys whose parents ran a store across the street from our home in Atlanta. Then something began to happen. When I went across the street to get them, their parents would say they could not play. They weren't hostile; they just made excuses. Finally I asked my mother about it.

"Every parent at some time faces the problem of explaining the facts of life to his child. Just as inevitably, for the Negro parent, the moment comes when he must explain to his offspring the facts of segregation. My mother took me on her lap and began by telling me about slavery and how it ended with the Civil War. She tried to explain the divided system of the South—the segregated schools, restaurants, theatres, housing; the white and colored signs on drinking fountains, waiting rooms and lavatories—as a social condition rather than a natural order. Then she said the words that every Negro hears before he can yet understand the injustice that makes them necessary: 'You are as good as anyone.'"

Their lives were young and tender then. At their ages Malcolm and Martin should have been romping and shouting with happy laughter, playing as healthy children do. And they both did play, yet America's racist society had already shadowed their lives. The social foces that rose up to fleck the lives of both youngsters are cardinal guidelines from the syllabus on how to kill a black man.

The first and imperative step is to, at an early age, compromise the male-child's view of his father as a man basically in control of his own life—as a father thus able to make the lives of his children secure. In the case of Malcolm the compromise was total; his father was abused, harrassed and, finally, killed. Martin's father, by contrast, was completely a professional success. Yet he was a "boy" to the policeman and the simple act of buying shoes produced a racial incident. Both approaches are variants of the same basic tactic, an exercise in the act and art of killing black men.

TWO

THE EDUCATION OF MALCOLM

Malcolm X began his education at integrated Pleasant Grove School when he was five years old and one year before his father's murder. The Littles were the only black family in the community and there were no incidents accompanying their attendance at the school. Malcolm was later to laugh as he commented that white people don't resent Negroes in their midst as long as there are too few Negroes there to pose a threat. Even so the white students called Malcolm and his brothers and sisters such names as "nigger," "darkie," and "Rastus." Nobody, including the Littles, felt there was anything wrong or unusual about this. There is little, if any, recorded material concerning Malcolm's school experiences for the years between 1931 and 1937. It is clear that with the death of his father he became absorbed in the problems and poverty of his family and his school record was sullied, both in terms of academics and character. He was caught stealing several times during that period and the record shows that his deportment was such that he lived every school day on the brink of being expelled. A 1937 classroom incident provides a clear insight into what had happened to Malcolm both in school and in the streets.

In June of that year Joe Louis filled every black youngster with pride as he defeated James Braddock to become the heavyweight champion of the world. Millions of young Negroes suddenly saw themselves as boxing champions and dreamed of entering the ring as a path to glory. Malcolm's ring debut was against a white youth who floored young Malcolm some fifty times before being declared the victor. Malcolm was an outcast in the black community because he had been defeated in the ring by a white man. It was a few days later that Malcolm entered the classroom with his hat on. The white teacher ordered Malcolm to walk around the room with his hat on until ordered to stop. "That way," the teacher said, "everyone can see you. Meanwhile, we'll go on with class for those who are here to learn something."

Malcolm's future may well have been altered if the white teacher had paused to learn something—why Malcolm wore his hat inside the classroom. But, and this was a key factor in shaping the lives of so many Negroes in the non-South, the teacher simply punished anyone who varied from the white, middle class norm. Perhaps this is hindsight sociology and psychology but it was clear that the wearing of his hat was Malcolm's symbolic way of reaffirming his manhood. It is a common practice among the black masses and is rooted in the Southern tradition that demanded that the Negro man always take off his hat in the presence of white people. In an extreme counterraction, then, Negro males tend to wear their hats in places and at times that offend general etiquette.

Malcolm continued to walk around the room as ordered, but when the teacher rose from his chair to write on the blackboard Malcolm put a tack in his chair with predictable results. So predictable were the results, in fact, that Malcolm was suspended and sent to reform school. He was then thirteen years old. Malcolm endeared himself to his

white "keepers" despite the fact that they constantly used such words as "niggers" and "coons." It was
a tribute to both their missionary spirit and Malcolm's genius with people that the white "keepers"
of the reform school arranged for Malcolm to attend the local junior high school, a privilege that no
other ward of the reform school had enjoyed.

It was at Mason Junior High that Malcolm discovered the magic of history even though his history
teacher explained the Civil War period by singing
"some folks say a nigger won't steal, I caught one in
my cotton field;" and the teacher added the aside,
"niggers' feet are so big that when they run they
don't leave tracks, they leave holes in the ground."
Malcolm became fascinated with English as well; he
was fortunate enough to have a teacher who talked
to him privately about making a man of himself.
Malcolm turned out to be the campus pet; he was
elected to the debating team and made president of
his class. He was a varsity member of the basket-
ball team and led his squad to victory as the white
crowds shouted "nigger," "coon," and "ape."

But Malcolm was also undergoing another kind
of learning during this time. He made periodic trips
to visit with his brothers and sisters in Lansing; at
night he spent his time in the bars and honky-tonks
of the black ghetto. A strong and agile youth, in
more ways than one, Malcolm seems to have been
mastering both worlds, that of the white school and
that of the Negro ghetto. One could have easily
predicted that he would overcome his difficult beginning and become a black professional, perhaps a
lawyer, but two events were to irrevocably alter the
course of Malcolm's education.

The first occurrence was the much heralded visit
of Malcolm's sister, Ella Collins, who lived in Bos-

ton, Massachusetts. Ella was Malcolm's half-sister. She was something of a legend in the family, since for years the Little children had listened to stories about Ella, the commanding black woman who lived in Boston, mixed with the Negro middle class and owned property. Ella's visit resulted in a family reunion that climaxed when they all visited Malcolm's mother who was still confined to the mental institution. But there was more. Ella questioned Malcolm about his progress in school and then offered him a trip to Boston for the summer of 1940. That was the second event that was to change things. For the first time in his life Malcolm saw something approaching a stable and respectable Negro society—lavishly furnished Negro churches and well appointed black homes. Interracial couples walked hand in hand through the streets of Roxbury, the Negro district of Boston, something Malcolm dared not do back home in Lansing and Mason. It was a new world for Malcolm and even as he absorbed it Malcolm had the deep feeling that Thomas Wolfe was correct, a man can never go home again.

Malcolm did go back home for September and the beginning of school. But things were never the same. Out of a monumental misreading of the black world he had visited in Boston he began to recoil from the white world that was his classroom and reform school. Although he continued to do excellent work his teachers soon noticed that he was withdrawn; he spoke only when spoken to. That was not like Malcolm.

Then came the final blow. Malcolm had been deeply impressed by the black professionals whom he saw and met in Boston. He even then realized his facility with words and his ability to move an audience. Malcolm arranged a private conference with his English teacher and faculty advisor.

"I have been thinking," Malcolm said to the white teacher. "I have decided I want to be a lawyer."

The instructor reacted as if he had been impaled by a spear. "You are a good student," the teacher replied, "but it is time for you to face the reality that you are a nigger. A lawyer! That is not a realistic goal for a nigger. You need to start thinking about something you can be. You are good with your hands," the faculty advisor continued, "you are good at making things. Why don't you plan on carpentry? People like you personally; you will get lots of work."

It was an exchange Malcolm would never forget. Malcolm never quite forgave himself for not ignoring the white faculty advisor and pursuing his professional dream. And much of Malcolm's strident criticism of Negro professionals in his mature years was rooted in his inward frustration over an unfulfilled dream.

Malcolm grew even more sullen and quiet, in the classroom, in the restaurant where he washed dishes, and at the reform school. He was no longer the kind of Negro white people enjoyed having around; they could not understand him. It was a self-serving ploy for all concerned when Malcolm was paroled from the reform school and sent to Lansing to live with a Negro family. Malcolm grew even more introspective, and his half-sister Ella did not relieve the situation when she arranged for Malcolm to be paroled to her. The week Malcolm completed the eighth grade, he boarded the Greyhound bus for Boston.

Ella Collins was a strong and domineering woman but her dream of controlling young Malcolm could not have been more in vain. It took the perceptive Malcolm less than a month to realize that the black society he saw in Boston was but a façade covering the same social and family weaknesses he had known in the ghetto of Lansing. The scorn he had developed for the Lansing middle class black rushed to the fore, and Malcolm dismissed the Boston black elite with disdain and made his bed with the hustlers, pimps, whores, and high livers. There was a poignant and tragic moment when a scholarly, Christian black girl fell in love with Malcolm—the hustler and soda jerk. She wanted so much to save him. Instead he pulled her down, brutalized her, then left her to wallow in the gutter as a whore and dope addict.

Malcolm's classrooms were the bars, dance halls, dope dens, and whorehouses of both New York and Boston. His major interests were dancing "the big apple," pimping for prostitutes, stealing, and both pushing and using dope. They called him "Big Red" to distinguish him from "Detroit Red," the now famous comedian Redd Foxx. The long, lanky Big Red cut a wide swath across New York and lower New England. Many writers have dismissed Malcolm's days as a hustler as just so much hell-raising. I submit that there is a good deal more to be said than that.

I knew Malcolm well. He was a brilliant man and could have made it. He didn't want to make it; he wanted to outwit it. After all a hustler is a man who somehow manages to make the money that supposedly accrues to only the God loving, hard working, white middle class, by employing methods that violate all of the middle class laws, and with a glee that informs the white middle class precisely where they can shove their value system. Many of Malcolm's contemporaries are still Harlem hustlers; they are now as he once was—individuals so alienated that they elect to make their way outside the boundaries of our society. They suffer neither the drudgery of nine-to-five work by day nor the visit of the income tax man by night. They are among those whom the census takers never count, for legally they do not exist. Yet they are there; they wield amazing influence in both politics and community economics. They live the life a hedonistic sultan without any fear of the heart attacks that seize struggling white middle class males, and with a total non-knowing of the hunger and despair that attend the black masses. These men never surface to challenge the white establishment; their sub rosa existences depend upon things remaining just as they are. This well could have been Malcolm's fate, to live and die as a hustler. But society arrested him for stealing and sentenced him to ten years in prison, to a place where he had no alternative but to spend his long nights reading and thinking. History may record that this was one of the biggest mistakes white law enforcement ever made.

Malcolm's prison years are now discussed in mystical terms by those who elevated him to sainthood and martyrdom. The harsh truth is that these years of confinement allowed Malcolm to crystallize the forces that were already at work within him. The Black Muslim doctrine capsulated his experience with white people, women, poverty, crime, and Christianity. I see no moral or intellectual magic in Malcolm's acceptance of the thesis that all white men are devils; and is there a substantive difference between a man who pimps for prostitutes and a Black Muslim brother who orders his wife to walk several steps behind him? Is it shocking that a man whose father, a baptist minister, had been murdered by whites, should discover that Christianity is a failure? What objective observer can be surprised when a man of Malcolm's background becomes a fire-and-brimestone prophet spelling out the impending doom of the white institutions he is convinced are responsible for his own agonizing plight? What psychiatrist would expect Malcolm to do other than to embrace a father-teacher image who preaches a doctrine that sums up all of Malcolm's crystallized thoughts?

On the Sunday before Labor Day in 1952, Malcolm Little, who had been out of prison on parole only a few weeks, was received by The Honorable Elijah Muhammad, the leader of the Black Muslims and Malcolm's father image-to-be. Early in January of 1953, Malcolm gave up his job in order to devote more time to the Black Muslim movement, and that summer he made the journey to the pulpit as he became Assistant Minister of Temple Number One in Detroit.

The same summer, 1953, Martin Luther King, Jr. also made a journey that led to the pulpit. After nineteen continuous years in school young Martin had completed the requirements for a Ph.D. at Boston College, just a few miles from where Malcolm was imprisoned. Martin was uncertain about his future. There was that in him that wanted to preach; the rest of him wanted to teach. He elected to journey from Atlanta to Montgomery, Alabama, and give a trial sermon in the then vacant pulpit of the Dexter Avenue Baptist Church. Young Martin's topic was "The Three Dimensions of a Complete Life." He, like everybody else, had no idea what would happen next.

THREE

THE PULPIT

Martin Luther King, Jr.'s automobile journey from Atlanta to Montgomery in late August of 1953 was a trek to the inevitable. After nineteen continuous years of schooling Martin was now in search of both a professional beginning and his male independence. Martin was then twenty-three years old; he was married and had completed all of the requirements for his doctorate at Boston University but for the writing of his dissertation. For four years—since he was nineteen, that is—Martin had co-pastored the Ebenezer Baptist Church with his father; during the summer vacations Martin had assumed the entire pastoral load while his father and mother retreated to Europe and the Holy Land. Young Martin was not a man in need of a job; to the contrary he was a man with so many opportunities open to him that decision making was his most difficult problem. He could remain as co-pastor of Ebenezer with his father. But this would have meant remaining under his father's shadow, under the thumb of one of the most dominating men the Southern Negro subculture has produced. At least four college posts were Martin's for the taking that day when he took the fateful drive from Atlanta to Montgomery. Martin did wish to pursue the life of Academia, but there was the preacher in him, that part of him that needed to mount the pulpit, stand where Isaiah stood and eloquently thunder out man's sins while pointing to the cross of Calvary as the only redemptive way out. Had Malcolm X and Martin Luther King, Jr. met each other at that moment in 1953, each could have denounced the other as totally unfit to guide or lead their people. Both would have been convinced that the other's way could only lead to greater enslavement. Their lives and the forces that produced these two martyrs were that much in opposition at that time.

Martin was to the black manor born; he was to cast his lot with the poor—black and white—because of a dedication that only can be described as a combination of moral commitment and missionary zeal. Malcolm was to the ghetto born, yet he was nurtured on the vision of middle class goodies; he was to become a zealot against the black middle class people partly because they conspired with white racism as well as because they enjoyed all of the luxuries he once almost had. The pulpit was the inevitable platform for both men.

For Martin Luther King, Jr., the journey from Atlanta led to the pastorate of the Dexter Avenue Baptist Church of Montgomery. Not only is the city of Montgomery the seat of the old Confederacy, but the Dexter Avenue Baptist Church encapsulates what happened to the Negro during the era of Reconstruction; it is a congregation of middle class black educated people. For the most part they are sedate and unemotional; not only do they pride themselves on the fact that most of the congregation is light skinned, but they are not the much publicized "shouting niggers" of Southern black Baptist churches who are still apt to kick over benches and throw things when the spirit of the Lord comes down upon them. They and Martin

were well met. He was out of the black South's best
stock and a Ph.D. out of Boston University as well;
they were blood of his blood, flesh of his flesh,
school teachers and professionals.

For Malcolm, the road from prison led to the
co-ministership of Elijah Muhammad's Mosque
Number One in Detroit. These Black Muslims and
Malcolm were well met; they were a congregation
of the disillusioned and the defeated, women who
had lost faith in the Christian proposition and men
who found the Black Muslim dogma an overcoming
of prison records. Both Malcolm and Martin had
been properly educated, and in the right institutions, for the roles they were to play.

For the first several months of his pastorate at
Dexter Avenue Baptist Church, Martin Luther King
commuted between Boston and Montgomery one
weekend every month. Only after he had completed
his doctorate did he assume full-time pastorship of
the church. Malcolm X commuted every night between his job as a salesman in a white owned
furniture store in the black ghetto of Detroit and
Mosque Number One, some twenty blocks away.
The gospels they preached were as dissimilar as
their travel patterns, yet they both were laying the
foundations of their work as evangelical revolutionaries.

The preaching role of the early Martin Luther
King was to comfort the comfortable, not to disturb
them. When he stood in the pulpit of the Dexter
Avenue Baptist Church for the first time, he was
indecisive as to whether he should court the
congregation's intellectuality by giving a sermon of
some profound theological theme, or deliver the
kind of emotional and inspirational message that is
so typical of black Baptists in the Deep South.

Martin, in his own words, elected to "put God out front and keep Martin Luther King in the background." His initial message, "The Three Dimensions of a Complete Life," turned out to be a black Southern intellectual's *tour de force*; it was a high call for man to enlarge his mental, spiritual, and physical life, a call for men to think clearly, love the Lord, and walk briskly. The sermon was rooted in Christian theology, of course, but it was the kind of pietistic homily that encourages the virtues of inward devotion and good works. Like the sermons that were being delivered in Christian churches all over the South that Sunday morning, Martin's message invoked an unplugging of the pipeline that runs from the individual to God. There was nothing about his message, if delivered by white clergymen, that would cause the parishioners to go out and be more decent to their black neighbors on Monday morning. By the same taken there was nothing in what Martin preached that day that would cause the members of his congregation to take up picket signs and march the streets. Martin's ultimate point was that love is the only redemptive power; his sermon was the script for an inward closet drama that everyone should act out on Sunday afternoon with no obligation to go out and change society on Monday morning. But the revolutionary element in what Martin preached lay in the fact that he led people to make a moral commitment from which they could not retreat once their vows of love and brotherhood were put to test.

Malcolm's gospel was raw, real, and rasping. God is black and He made black men in His image, thus it is that all black men are by nature good and all white men are by nature evil. Neither the white nor the black man had reason for either pride or guilt;

God, Allah, just made them that way. Not only was Christianity a false doctrine but it was a brainwashing theology concocted by the white man to keep black men in an inferior position. The American black man was the "lost and found in the wilderness of North America," a people in diaspora separated from their race—the blacks of the world, their religion—Islam, and their language—Arabic. All of the black man's ills, from public segregation to private immorality, were the results of the white devil's doings. More, Malcolm promised that when Elijah Muhammad gave the word there would be a worldwide, and violent, confrontation between God and the devil. The people said "Amen" because they knew that "God" is the black man collectively taken and the "devil" is the white man collectively taken. Thus the impending confrontation between God and the devil will be, in fact, a war between the blacks and whites of the world.

The early sermons of neither Malcolm X nor Martin Luther King are a matter of record. There are sermons and interviews that occurred later that reveal the kind of gospel both men were preaching in their early years as pulpiteers.

Asked to explain the refusal of Mrs. Rosa Parks to take a seat on the back of the bus, Martin King replied, "she has been tracked down by the *Zeitgeist*—the spirit of the times." Negroes of Birmingham went on to launch a boycott of busses because of Mrs. Parks' ordeal and Martin King made this comment about the effort:

"Every rational explanation breaks down at some point. There is something about the protest that is superrational; it cannot be explained without a divine dimension. Some may call it a principle of correction, with Alfred N. Whitehead; or a process of integration, with Henry N. Wieman; or Being-It-self, with Paul Tillich; or a personal God."

Martin Luther King was describing socio-racial events in the language one hears at Crozier Theological Seminary and Boston University. But Malcolm X described the same events in the language one learns in the jungles of the ghetto and the prison yard:

"When I say the white man is a devil," Minister Malcolm shouted, "I speak with the authority of history."

"That's right," the people shout back.

"The record of history shows that the white men, as a people, have never done good."

"Say on, brother, say on."

"He stole our fathers and mothers from their culture of silk and satins, and brought them to this land in the belly of a ship—am I right or wrong?"

"You are right, God knows you are right."

"He brought us here in chains—right?"

"Right."

"He has kept us in chains ever since we have been here."

"Preach on, Brother Minister, preach on."

"Now this blue-eyed devil's time has about run out!"

The people leap to their feet, rejoicing.

"Now the fiery hell he has heaped upon others is about to come down on the white man!"

"All praise due to Allah," the people shout.

"God—we call him Allah—is going to get this white, filthy, hog-loving beast off our backs," Malcolm promises.

"Say on—yes, yes, yes . . ."

"God is going to hitch him to the plow and make him do his own dirty work."

"Yes, yes. Say on!"

"God is going to take over the garment district and make those white dogs push their own trucks."

Men in the audience jump up and down and shout their approval: "All praises due to Allah. Praise His holy name!"

"Now, now," Malcolm says, "calm down, because I want you to hear me. Now I want to tell you who God is. I want you to understand who Allah is so you will know who is going to get this white, dope-peddling beast off your back."

Malcolm smiles. A ripple of laughter runs through the audience—you see, they know who Allah is; they know who God is; they know just who is going to get the white man off their backs. But they have come to hear Malcolm "make it plain" again.

"The Honorable Elijah Muhammad teaches us that God—Allah—is not a spook; we don't worship any ghost for a God. We don't believe in any dead God."

"That's right."

"Our God is a live God."

"Yes."

"He is walking around here with you, among you, in you."

"Yes," the people shout back.

"God is black like you; He walks with you; He talks like you ..."

By this time, the people are back on their feet cheering. But Malcolm has gone as far toward describing God as he will go for a while.

Both Malcolm and Martin were serving their congregations well. Martin was extolling a gospel that defined the black man's plight in the classical terms of Paul Tillich, and the clear implication was that the ultimate resolution would come by divine intervention. Malcolm's definition of the problem was in language that reflected as much of the gutter as one could import to the Temple. His resolution was also in divine terms; but his God was the black cook who would one day poison her "white family" and the black man who would one day shout "Burn, Baby, Burn!"

And as they preached from their respective pulpits in 1953 neither dreamt, nor hoped, that events would force them out of the pulpit and into the arena of racial leadership.

FOUR

THE ZEITGEIST

The spirit of the times overtook both Martin Luther King, Jr. and Malcolm X. Whatever their private ambitions may have been, they both were catapulted beyond the pulpit into an arena of racial leadership, and into the kind of dynamic activity that would lead them to fame, criticism, death, and martyrdom.

Martin spent the first eighteen months of his pastorate getting to know his congregation and his town. As King well knew before he assumed the pastorate, the Dexter Avenue church did not enjoy a good reputation among Montgomery's black masses; it was contemptuously referred to as "the silk stocking" and "big folks" church. The plain implication was that nonprofessional and uneducated Negroes were not welcomed at the Dexter Avenue altar. This impression was not without foundation in fact. Indeed, historians will find interest in the fact that The Reverend Vernon Johns, Martin's predecessor at Dexter Avenue, came to Montgomery after pastoring the Berea Baptist Church of Washington, D.C. Nestled close to Howard University, Berea church was notorious for its discrimination against dark skinned and working class Negroes. During my student days at American University in Washington, the standing joke was that the officers of Berea church hung a fine tooth comb in the entrance each Sunday morning; any

Negro whose hair became entangled in the comb
would not be allowed to enter and worship.

It was this class discrimination in his own church,
then, that first demanded Martin's attention. He
launched a "whosoever will" program, an effort
designed to make Dexter Avenue a spiritual haven
for all, regardless of class, who wished to come in
and worship. But Dexter Avenue was only sympto-
matic of Montgomery itself. Segregation was a way
of life, an institution accepted and obeyed by both
white and black. Some two years before Martin
assumed the pastorate of Dexter Avenue Church,
The Reverend Vernon Johns was ordered to move
to the rear of the bus by the white driver. Johns
refused to move and when ordered off the bus,
demanded that his fare be refunded; the entire
matter broke into a shouting match between Johns
and the driver and at the peak of the argument
Johns called for all the Negroes on the bus to walk
off with him. Not only did the Negroes remain in
their seats, but one member of Dexter Avenue
Church rebuked Johns for his actions, saying "you
should know better!"

As Martin himself described it, the Montgomery
of 1954 was a deeply divided city; the educated
Negroes were indifferent, the uneducated Negroes
were passive, and Negro leadership was made impotent by factionalism. Martin King encountered
his first criticism in Montgomery because he joined
both the NAACP and the Alabama Council On
Human Relations. The NAACP was then wedded
to the philosophy that segregation could only be
ended by recourse to new legislation and appeals to
the courts, The Council was an interracial organization motivated by the assumption that only through
education could the races come to love and under-

stand each other. Martin's critics accused him of having dual loyalties, commitments to two organizations whose approaches to the race problem were different. Martin's statement of defense was indeed prophetic:

"This question betrays the assumption that there (is) only one approach to the solution of the race problem. On the contrary, I feel that both approaches are necessary. Through education we seek to change attitudes, through legislation and court orders we seek to regulate behavior."

Martin continued his relationship with both organizations and, after a long talk with his wife, he refused the presidency of the NAACP in 1955. In March of that year Claudette Colvin, a fifteen-year-old high school girl, refused to surrender her bus seat to a white passenger and the driver ejected her from the vehicle; she was handcuffed, manhandled, and taken to jail. The Negro community formed a committee to make protests to the proper authorities. Martin Luther King was a member of the committee. The group met with J. E. Begley, manager of the Montgomery Bus Lines, and Dave Bormingham, then police commissioner. Begley admitted the driver was wrong in having Miss Colvin arrested and promised to take action against the driver. Bormingham said he would order the City Attorney to issue a definite policy statement concerning bus seating. The Negro committee left the meeting with hope, but their white conferees proceeded to do the exact opposite of what they had promised. The City Attorney never issued the clarifying statement and the young Negro girl was convicted and given a suspended sentence.

Tension over the busses continued to mount during the summer and fall of 1955, and the arrest that

Martin was to later call "decisive" occurred on December first of that year. The story has been written thousands of times: Mrs. Rosa Parks, a seamstress, refused to yield her seat to a white male passenger. She was quietly arrested and for several hours few people knew of the incident. It was actually a few women connected with the Women's Political Council who set things in motion through a series of telephone calls. Martin King did not hear of the incident until the following morning, Friday, when he received a phone call from E. D. Nixon. By mid-afternoon an ad hoc committee had been formed and the call to boycott the busses was issued. Since the boycott was to go into effect the following Monday morning, the committee devoted much of its time devising plans to inform the black community of the protest. Leaflets were hastily mimeographed and distributed in the Negro neighborhood, but the group got a lusty assist from a totally unexpected quarter. The events surrounding this unexpected assistance gave Martin one of his funniest stories, a true tale he would tell with gestures and gusto during relaxed private moments. In essence this is what happened: A Negro maid, who was totally illiterate, found one of the boycott leaflets on her front porch when she came home from work on Friday. Unable to read the leaflet she took it to work Saturday and asked her white "Lady" what it was all about. The "Lady" grew incensed, picked up the phone and called the *Montgomery Advertiser*, that city's powerful newspaper and a bastion of segregation, to advise the editors "what the uppity niggers are doing." The paper ran a major story informing white people that the Negroes were about to get out of line. The story also informed thousands of Negroes who would not

have known about the boycott that the protest was
being planned.

It was a moving moment for Martin and his wife,
Coretta, as they stood in their living room on
Monday morning and watched the empty busses
roll by. The boycott was amazingly effective. As
Martin was to later describe it, "the black folks
were walking to work and praising the Lord!" That
night there was another moving moment in the
King household, one that was to change the course
of Martin's life.

Certain that the boycott was going well, Martin
King and other Negro leaders left the streets late
Monday morning to attend the trial of Mrs. Rosa
Parks. She was, of course, convicted and fined ten
dollars plus court costs—a total of fourteen dollars.
At three o'clock that afternoon the Negro leaders
held a meeting to structure their organization and
prepare for a mass rally to be held Monday evening. After the afternoon meeting Martin went
home, and he and his wife began to exchange
information about the day's events. Then Martin
said:

"I was elected president of the movement."

"You know," Coretta replied, "whatever you do
you have my backing."

A hasty reading of history would lead to the
conclusion that it was at this moment, his election
to the presidency of the Montgomery Improvement
Association, that the spirit of the time overtook
Martin Luther King, Jr. I think not: the most logical
prediction at that point would have been that King
would lead the boycott movement to partial success
and then return to the anonymity of the pulpit. He
did not return to the pulpit, and the *why* of his
nonreturn is the key to his martyrdom.

It must be recalled that the Montogmery bus boycott occurred during a generally tense period in American race relations. The Supreme Court's school desegregation decision had been announced in May of 1954, and there had been sporadic violence at several Southern colleges undergoing "integration" including the University of Alabama. Television was then in its infancy, but Martin Luther King provided TV newsmen with an ideal hero figure upon whom they could focus as the racial drama unfolded. He was young, educated, eloquent, and an always willing subject. His face and his cause became common fare in millions of homes across the nation. This was also the era during which major newspapers began to hire Negro reporters. For the first time white readers in New York, Chicago, and other sections of the North, read reports of race conflicts in the South written by black reporters, most of whom had been born and educated in the South. Carl Rowan came to Birmingham from Minneapolis, Ted Poston came in from New York, and I came in from Chicago; although we remained objective about the facts of the conflict there was no doubt that we supported the boycott in general and Martin as a leader-personality. Indeed, there were few white reporters, excluding those from the Deep South, who did not feel and write as we did. It is no detraction from Martin to say that but for the news media he would have remained an unsung clergyman.

The projection of Martin also occurred at a time when the civil rights movement was desperately in need of a hero image. Despite the magnificent legal battle waged by the NAACP, neither the organization nor Roy Wilkins, its Executive Director had the charisma, the force, so essential to the folk-hero

syndrome. It was as if Martin had been chiseled out
of the black mountain to make an eternal liar out of
white people. White people argued that Negroes
were stupid; there was Martin with his Ph.D. in his
mid-twenties. White people alleged that Negroes
were lazy, unable to organize and accomplish a
objective; Martin not only was hard working, but
he pulled together an organization that put thousands of people to walking for justice, and he
sustained the movement for more than a year.
White people stereotyped Negroes as men of violence, yet Martin mounted the only nonviolent social revolution in Western history. Most of all,
Martin's public speeches combined the wisdom of
Socrates, the eloquence of Demosthenes, and the
thunder of Isaiah. One could not have created a
black man who could have better filled the nation's
television screens. Even as I talked to Martin during the early days of Montgomery, we both realized
it would be all but impossible for him to return to
the pastorate, the pastorate alone. What we did not
realize was that certain white men and events
would make the choice for him.

But for a brief paragraph in his book *Stride
Toward Freedom,* little had been said or written
about the impact a white, segregationist, Baptist
minister had on Martin's thinking and subsequent
behavior. Having discussed this with Martin on
several occasions, I am convinced that Dr. E.
Stanley Frazier, then minister to the all white St.
James Methodist Church in Montgomery, had a
decisive effect on Martin's decision. It was a brief
encounter, this hostile dialogue between Martin
King and Dr. Frazier, but it was the kind of
high moment that changes lives. The Mayor of
Montgomery had convened a group of both black

and white citizens to find a way to end the boycott, then two weeks old. Dr. Frazier was an open and ardent segregationist, and he took the floor to not only denounce the boycott, but to excoriate Martin personally. As Martin recalled it, Dr. Frazier lashed out at the black clergymen for leading the boycott when their Christian calling demanded that they should be leading their congregations in meditation about "the babe born in Bethlehem."

Martin was then just out of seminary and his fury over what Frazier said forced him into one of the few intemperate outbursts of his short life. Martin's anger over what he felt was Frazier's anti-Negro posture was surpassed only by his dismay over what he felt was a total prostitution of the Christian ethic. Even Martin's black supporters, including Ralph Abernathy, were stunned as Martin usurped the floor and erupted:

"We, too, know the Jesus the minister referred to," he began. "We have had an experience with Him, and we believe firmly in the revelation of God in Jesus Christ. I can see no conflict between our devotion to Jesus Christ and our present action. In fact, I see a necessary relationship," he continued, "(for) if one is truly devoted to Jesus, he will seek to rid the world of social evils."

It is clear to me—and I am certain that the publication of his private papers will confirm this—that this experience, and others like it, led Martin to conclude that racism was endemic to the Christian church, particularly in the South. His moment in history was that of a Negro leader, but I suggest that his basic role was that of a prophet who sought to purge the church of its sins.

Nor was Martin's indictment against the church lodged against the white church alone; he felt that

the black's churches in action were as ungodly as
the white church's espousal of segregation. During
his student days Martin had been deeply influenced
by the writings of moral activists, including Karl
Marx, and even as early as the first days of the
Montgomery boycott it was evident that he himself
would desert the pulpit for the activist's role:

"It has been affirmed that any change in present
conditions would mean going against the cherished
customs of our community," he said in rebuttal to
Dr. Frazier. "But if the customs are wrong we have
every reason to change them. The decision that we
must now make is whether we will give our alle-
giances to outmoded and unjust customs or the
ethical demands of the universe. As Christians we
owe our allegiance to God and His will rather than
to men and his folkways."

I feel it was inevitable that the man behind these
words, particularly since he had been given an
international platform through the press, would one
day soon found a civil rights organization based on
Christian ideas and rooted in the church. He was
deeply convinced that the church must first purge
itself of racism and then go on to purge all of
society. This was to put him in sharp conflict with
those civil rights groups that were more securely
based. But he was to persist in this to the end.
Indeed, at his death he was forging a movement of
black churchmen, the purpose of which was to
wrest control of the North's black ghettos from the
advocates of violence and black power.

Martin Luther King was less than two years into
his career as a pastor when he was called upon to
lead the Montgomery bus boycott movement. It
was almost inevitable that he would enter the ministry after a childhood so dominated by his power-

ful father, Martin King, Sr. Few people know that both he and his father were named "Michael King" at birth and that their names were changed when Martin was seven years old to "Martin Luther," in honor of the great leader of the Reformation. While a student at Morehouse College, Martin fell under the tutelage and personal influence of Dr. Benjamin Mays, then President of Morehouse and a close friend of Dr. King, Sr. Dr. Mays, himself a Baptist minister, is credited with having given Martin the final shove that directed him toward the ministry.

Even so, not all of Martin wanted to preach. In both his writings and during his private moments he spoke of his longing for scholarship, of his deep desire to return to the classroom. From private talks with him I am convinced that his ultimate dream was to head a major university. Had he not become a civil rights leader he almost certainly would have realized this dream. During the last five years of his life the presidencies of both Howard and Morehouse universities became vacant. He was prominently mentioned for both posts but his work as a civil rights activist caused the posts to elude him. Even so, the pulpit of the Dexter Avenue Church was much too narrow a platform for Martin. His intellect was stifled, his love for a more liberal social life was thwarted. I agree with those who say that had he not become involved with the civil rights movement he would have left Dexter Avenue for the university campus in a matter of time, say five years.

One must view Martin's assumption of the leadership of the Montgomery Improvement Association, then, as his final growing up. Had he not done that he would have done something else. The pulpit was not big enough to hold him. It was also Mar-

tin's additional movement away from his strong-
willed father, his movement to even more become
his own man. I am not suggesting open conflict
between Martin and his father, but I am calling
attention to the fact that such men as Martin
Luther King, Sr. are so strong and hard driving that
they traditionally are all but impossible to live with.
Such men tend to confuse their own desires with
God's will and the sons who bear their names spend
the first quarter of their lives trying to establish
their own manhood in a manner that will not
alienate their fathers. The ideal thing, from the
elder King's point of view, would have been for
Martin, Jr. to remain in Atlanta as his father's
co-pastor; instead Martin moved to Montgomery as
pastor of Dexter Avenue. Once there the ideal
thing, again from the father's point of view, would
have been for Martin to stay in his pulpit; instead
Martin moves into the social arena and accepts the
leadership of the Montgomery Improvement Association. Little has been said or written about this,
but some documented evidence is available.

The boycott is several months old. Martin is at
Fisk University in Nashille, Tennessee, for a series
of lectures and he has left his wife and child with
his parents in Atlanta. The word is flashed by radio
and television that all of the boycott leaders, including Martin, have been indicted by a grand jury
and are to be arrested the following morning. Martin quits his Fisk lectures and flies to Atlanta; his
intention is to gather his family and then fly to
Montgomery and surrender. Dr. King, Sr. inter-
venes. He does not wish Martin to return; he is
afraid for his son's life. In an extraordinary move
that is destined to become a classic insight into
Negro social organization, King, Sr. convenes a

meeting of prominent Atlanta Negroes, including Dr. Benjamin Mays, to discuss whether Martin should return to Montgomery. King, Sr. opens the meeting by saying that Martin should not return to Montgomery; sounds of "Amen" ripple across the living room of the Ebenezer Baptist Church parsonage. Martin remains silent as his parents and his peers debate his future. The record indicates that even Dr. Benjamin Mays opposed Martin's return. Then came the moment of umbilical severance:

"I must go back to Montgomery," Martin, Jr. told that assembly of the concerned, "my friends and associates are being arrested. It would be the height of cowardice for me to stay away. I would rather be in jail for ten years than desert my people now. I have begun the struggle, and I can't turn back. I have reached the point of no return."

The Zeitgeist had now overtaken Martin Luther King, Jr. Not only did he return to Montgomery but his father drove him there and remained with him through the ordeals of bombing, jailings, and personal harassment that were to follow. Only another Negro male born in the same social mold, as I was, can fully understand what that moment meant to Martin, Jr. Not only did he make a high commitment to something he passionately believed in but, in the same process, he won his freedom from his father and his dignity as a man. And it came in a manner that allowed him to remain his father's best and closest friend. Not all of us who have defined our elders in search of both social freedom and personal independence have carried out that exercise with the same aplomb and come away as unscathed as young Martin did.

Martin and I grew up together although I am seven years his elder. My father (actually my uncle

who reared me) was to South Georgia what Martin
Luther King, Sr. was to Atlanta. He was—and is—a
powerful Baptist minister and educator. He was my
pastor on Sunday morning and my school principal
Monday through Friday. Not only is my father a
close friend of Dr. King, Sr. but it was he who, as
President of the Georgia Baptist Training Union
Convention, gave Martin, then in his early teens, his
first statewide platform on "Christian Youth" night.
I addressed the same convention. What I underline
here is not my personal relationship with Martin
(we were close friends) but the social history of the
era and area in which he lived and was murdered.
As I wrote in *The Negro Revolt* the black South
had a stout and healthy middle class society in
operation. We did not think of, nor did we wish for
a day when we would melt into the white society.
Martin's early days during the Montgomery bus
boycott make this clear. The Negroes made three
demands: Courteous treatment by the bus drivers,
the hiring of Negro drivers in predominantly Negro
areas and segregated seating, the Negroes seating
from the back toward the front and the whites
seating from the front toward the back on a first
come, first served basis. This was a compromise
that both King, Sr. and the white establishment
could have lived with. But the Zeitgeist was moving in yet another direction. King, Sr. had little
alternative but to drive his son back into Montgomery, and the Supreme Court decision that followed left Martin with no alternative but to support the concept of fully integrated busses. The bus
boycott was thus rendered a moot issue; Negroes
could sit where they pleased, even on the same seat
with white passengers.

This also meant that Martin Luther King, Jr. had

achieved an overwhelming success. His movements had ended bus segregation forever and his private fortitude had freed him from the shadow of his father. More, he was no longer the private property of the Dexter Avenue Baptist Church. He had already received several "Macedonian calls" from other black ministers in the deep South to come and help them execute the same social miracle in their towns. It is not surprising, then, that Martin convened a meeting of the "Southern Christian Leadership Council" in Atlanta to plan similar demonstrations in a spate of Southern cities. What is ironic is that this organizational meeting led to Martin's resignation of the pastorate of the Dexter Avenue Baptist Church in order to devote more time to the civil rights movement. The Zeitgeist had overcome.

FIVE

THE INTERVIEW

It is properly said that the news media played a large role in the projection of Martin Luther King and it can be even more properly said that the media projected Malcolm X into international prominence. I know this to be true because I did it.

It all started in the spring of 1959 and the account of the events as Malcolm X related them in his brilliant autobiography are totally false and distorted. I had then moved from Chicago to New York and was a member of Mike Wallace's staff, the first Negro ever to appear on television as a news reporter. I was living in Queens, a borough of New York City, and was not completely familiar with Harlem and the black nationalist fever that seizes that community every weekend. I was shocked, then, one Saturday night when I visited Harlem with a close friend, Robert Maynard (now a reporter for the Washington Post), and his white wife. Not only did the street corner orators denounce white people, particularly Jews, but Robert and his wife were treated with physical violence. On the following Monday morning I discussed the experience with my immediate superior on the Mike Wallace staff, Ted Yates, who was years later to be killed while covering the Israeli-Arab conflict in 1967 in Jerusalem. Ted and I shared my memorandum with Mike Wallace and we all agreed that Mike would not be able to air what I had seen and heard until I gathered enough hard proof to convince the policy makers of Channel 13, then Mike's host TV station. I remember it well—Ted rented a miniature tape recorder and I strapped it to my body for my return visit to Harlem the following Saturday night. I felt then, and even now I am convinced that I was correct, that had the black nationalists known I was taping their speeches, I would have been killed. Not only did I tape the speeches, but I managed to have private talks with such black nationalist leaders as Carlos Cook and James Lawson. As I sat in Chock-Full-o'-Nuts at the corner of 125th Street and Seventh Avenue, I was struck that they consistently referred to "Brother Malcolm X." When I asked who was Malcolm X, they replied that he was the local leader of the Black Muslims. And when I asked who, in God's name, were the Black Muslims they both broke with laughter.

After hearing my tape, Mike Wallace assigned me to begin work on a documentary that was later to be called "The Hate That Hate Produced." I had all but forgotten about the Black Muslim movement as the first few weeks of filming concentrated on James Lawson, Lewis Michaux, Carlos Cook, and other black nationalists. Even so, the name of Malcolm X kept recurring, and it was a close personal friend, Dr. Anna Hedgeman, who was then Administrative Assistant to Mayor Robert Wagner, who sternly told me that I had better interview Malcolm if I wanted a true picture of black national activity in Harlem.

I began my search for Malcolm by visiting the Temple Number Seven Restaurant along Lenox Avenue near 120th Street. My first contact was with a man called "Joseph X," Malcolm's closest confidant and head of the militant Fruit of Islam. He questioned me closely and then promised that I would get a "phone call." The call came two days later and Joseph told me to present myself at the restaurant at eleven o'clock the following morning. I presented myself and shared coffee with Joseph and three other men, all Black Muslims. Once again I underwent exhaustive questioning by Joseph and his Black Muslim cohorts. What I did not know at the moment was that one of the men was Malcolm X. After an hour Malcolm declared his identity and gave permission for the interview to continue. I sat stunned as the now familiar Black Muslim dogma fell from Malcolm's lips. Christianity was a racial fraud perpetuated by the white man who is a congenital devil and snake; black men are by nature good and will one day destroy the white man. Oscillating between Masonic and Islamic thought, Malcolm went on to say that the only hope for the black man was to separate himself from the white devils.

I asked Malcolm if he would consent to a filmed interview. He made it clear that no interview could be granted without the consent of the Honorable Elijah Muhammad, the leader of the Black Muslim movement; he also told me that if the interview was granted I would have to conduct it, that he would never sit down with Mike Wallace, a white devil and a Jew. I elected to go for broke and asked Malcolm's intercession to obtain interviews on film with both Malcolm and Elijah Muhammad. In his autobiography, Malcolm gives a completely false account of the subsequent events. His misstatements are of the head, not the heart; by then he and I had become close friends and I know that his distortion of the facts grew out of the mental strain of his last two years, the period during which he dictated his autobiography to a mutual friend, Alex Haley. This aside may be of interest. During the time Malcolm was dictating his autobiography to Alex, I was writing my book *When The Word Is Given,* an in-depth study of the Black Muslim movement. I secluded myself in a downtown New York hotel and had no inkling that after Malcolm visited me for in-depth interviews that he was quietly taking the elevator to another floor where Alex Haley was closeted. Nor did Alex know where I was and what I was doing. I all but discovered Malcolm's double life when David Brown, then my editor at New American Library, expressed a desire to use a certain picture I had of Malcolm on the jacket of the book. I discussed the matter with Malcolm and he said he would have to make sure the use of the picture would not disturb "something else that is in progress." I did not know what the "something else" was and prudently did not press the issue. The picture is now on the flyleaf of that book.

In his autobiography, Malcolm says that following our meeting in the Temple Number Seven Restaurant I flew to Chicago to get Elijah's permission to film the two interviews. This is not true. Instead, Malcolm flew to Chicago and convinced Elijah that the interviews would be the best thing that ever happened to the Black Muslim movement. Mr. Muhammad agreed and I subsequently interviewed both men and filmed a Black Muslim meeting in Washington as well.

Nor was I the only Negro writer and social critic delving into the strange world of the Nation of Islam, the formal name of the Black Muslim movement. In 1958 Eric C. Lincoln, a professor of religion and sociology at Clark University in Atlanta, received an alarming term paper from one of his students. "The Christian religion is incompatible with the Negro's aspirations for dignity and equality in America," the paper began. "It has hindered where it might have helped; it has been evasive when it was morally bound to be forthright; it has separated believers on the basis of color, although it had declared its mission to be a universal brotherhood under Jesus Christ. Christian love is the white man's love for himself and for his race. For the man who is not white, Islam is the hope for justice and equality in the world we must build tomorrow."

Himself a Christian clergyman, Lincoln was startled by what he read. Investigation revealed that his student had become a convert to the Nation of Islam through the activity of the minister in charge of Temple Fifteen in Atlanta. Lincoln's curiosity and scholarship led him to obtain a grant and return to Boston University—where Martin King studied—and complete his doctorate; his dissertation was the first scholarly analysis of the Black Muslim movement. Lincoln and I crossed paths in 1959; he was researching his book and I was preparing the TV documentary. His book, *The Black Muslims In America*, is by far the most incisive study of that group. It was fortuitous for me that my reporter's eye caused me to concentrate on Malcolm X rather than on the Black Muslim organization itself. The Nation of Islam immediately struck me as being similar to several other sects and cults (Father Divine and Bishop Grace, for example) I had encountered. While a sophomore in college I had prepared a paper on Bishop Grace and I saw many of the same trappings in the Nation of Islam. But Malcolm X was gangling, awkward and a crude diamond that seemed certain to tumble out of the rough. He did indeed tumble out; maybe history will say that Lincoln and I pushed him out. Only time will tell.

The Nation of Islam was born in the black ghetto of Detroit during the murky and miserable days of the early thirties. Its founder was one W. D. Farad, a silk merchant from the East who spent his time teaching poor and illiterate Negroes an off-brand of Islam. The early records indicate that Farad attempted to restate the Islamic proposition in terms that would embrace the problems facing black Americans. The central myth, as Lincoln calls it, of Farad's doctrine was that God is black and made black men in his image; for a long time the black man lived in an Arabic Garden of Eden until a mad black scientist, Yacoub, began a genetic experiment. He interbred the lightest of black men until he manufactured a race of white devils. Few of Farad's disciples understood or cared about Yacoub and his dark doing. What did strike a note was Farad's broadside against Christianity. Farad branded Christianity the "white man's" religion and his allegation that the white Christian was nothing more than a devil found immediate validaton in the hearts of those black Detroiters who had just moved in from the Deep South. But there was more: The early records indicate that a number of Farad's followers were ex-Christians who, for one reason or the other, had grown angry with their church. To understand the import of this one must recall that the Southern Negro church was—and still is—oftimes the arena of bitter disputes and fights. The church was the only stable social institution Negroes had and the entire human drama of

leadership rivalry and social status was acted out in
that institution on Sunday morning. It was common
fare for ministers to be run out of town and for
deacons to shoot each other during prayer meetings. I recall clearly this scene from my childhood:
My grandfather, Thomas Lomax, pastored a church
in South Georgia and the congregation was kept in
a state of perpetual uproar because of two women
who were social rivals and hated each other's guts.
Both were deaconesses in our church—that is to say
their husbands were both deacons. During communion of a particular Easter Sunday the spirit of
the Lord just happened to strike one woman as she
was about to sip her communion wine. Without
spilling a drop of the wine the woman went into a
shout and holy-hopped her way clear across the
church and then had a divine spasm on the precise
spot that made it convenient for her to dump her
wine into the lap of her rival's new Easter dress.
Needless to say, church ended with a fight, not a
benediction. And it was the challenge to the minister to control such bitter factions as this that made
of Dr. Martin Luther King, Sr. the firm, but warm,
disciplinarian that he is; a father-trait that was to
play a major role in the shaping of Martin, Jr. The
point is that many of Farad's early followers came
from this sociological, subcultural base and their
willingness to approve a gospel that attacked Christianity may well have been rooted in some such
personal experience in the organized church. One
of Farad's early converts was Elijah Poole, a disillusioned ex-Baptist minister from Georgia.

There then followed a great deal of murky mysticism; supernatural noises rattled in coal bins, money disappeared, voices sounded up through the
ghetto sidewalk gratings, several key men in the

organization were found dead, and W. D. Farad simply vanished. The foul word "murder" has since then hung over the organization. One theory has it that Farad was indeed murdered and that his body was later discovered buried at an excavation sight. A new theory, one now being researched by two excellent black scholars, is that Farad fled to New York where he became active in the Garvey movement, the same back-to-Africa cult that had consumed Malcolm's father. When the mysticism was over, Elijah Poole had become The Honorable Elijah Muhammad and was the leader of the Black Muslim movement.

The accepted research indicates that the movement remained a rather small religious enclave with temples in Detroit and Chicago until the advent of Malcolm X some twenty years later. New evidence given to me in January of 1968 tends to confirm this theory, but a new dimension is added, one that provides a clearer insight into the motivations of Malcolm X.

The new information indicates that Ella Collins, Malcolm's strong willed half-sister, was closely allied with Elijah Muhammad in the early days. A deeply spiritual woman and believer in things mystical, Mrs. Collins was scheduled to become Muhammad's first female minister. Instead they fell into a dispute over organizational politics and money. Even so, Mrs. Collins and Elijah remained close friends and there is evidence that Muhammad took refuge in her Boston home during the days when fratracide seized the Black Muslim movement in Detroit.

This new information provides important links; it is now clear that Malcolm's early childhood was flecked by Elijah's influence. Malcolm's father lived

his last days in Lansing, some thirty miles from
Detroit. And it is certain that such an evangelical
black nationalist as Earl Little managed to journey
to Detroit and ponder the Black Muslim ideas
being taught by Farad and, then, Elijah Poole. This
assumption gathers even more strength now that
Ella Collins, Malcolm's sister, is strongly linked to
Elijah. Lincoln's research established that at least
two of Malcolm's brothers joined the Black Muslim
movement during those early years.

This, then, takes a good deal of the mysticism out
of Malcolm's conversion to Islam during his prison
years. The general assumption has been that Malcolm came upon the Black Muslim teachings while
in prison. It now appears, however, that Malcolm
had been familiar with the movement for several
years, and the solitary life of prison gave him time
to think and crystallize what had always been a
strong influence in his family life.

Malcolm had been Elijah's chief minister for
some five years when he and I first met. He had
graduated from the store front Mosque in Detroit
and gone on to become Muhammad's "Paul," the
evangelical missionary who toured the East Coast
establishing Mosques in every major city. Some two
months elapsed between the time I began filming
the documentary and when it was aired. Malcolm
would call me daily and tease, "You know the Devil
will not let you put that strong teaching on the air."
He was wrong. After editing the film, Mike Wallace, Ted Yates, and I carried out a battle of
attrition against the owners of the station until they
approved the airing of the project.

Starting on a Monday night, the documentary ran
a half hour for five nights as a part of Mike's hour
long newscast. Although we did not plan it this way,

the documentary ran the week preceding a Sunday rally the Black Muslims had scheduled at the St. Nicholas Arena in New York. The arena was packed hours before Elijah arrived and there occurred a memorable moment during Elijah's three hour sermon as he smilingly lashed out at Mike Wallace and me.

"Here, boy," he had Wallace saying to me on camera. "Wouldn't you say these Black Muslims are preaching hate?"

"Yassuh, boss, I sure am," I was made to reply.

But it was Malcolm the crowd had come to hear; for Malcolm, not Elijah, was the centerpiece of the documentary. And Malcolm did not fail them:

"Right," the people answered back.

"Our slave foreparents would have been put to death for advocating integration with the white man."

"Right; make it plain."

"Now when Mr. Muhammad speaks of 'separation,' the white man calls us 'hate teachers and facists.'"

"Speak, Brother Malcolm, speak."

"The white man doesn't want the blacks."

"Right, right, right!"

"And for the white man to ask the black man 'do you hate me' is just like the rapist asking the raped or the wolf asking the sheep 'do you love me!'"

"Make it plain, Brother Malcolm make it plain."

White reporters were not allowed to enter the arena but they stood outside and listened from loudspeakers as Malcolm indeed did make it plain. Within a fortnight every major magazine and news media was carrying long stories about the Black Muslims and particularly about Malcolm. Within a month Malcolm had received invitations to speak from every major university on the East Coast.

Malcolm had been catapulted into international fame, but he had also been cast in a role that would put him in sharp conflict with those close to Elijah and, eventually, with Elijah himself. That conflict certainly led to his assassination. There is yet another unpublished incident that provides insight into Malcolm's early fame.

In his autobiography, Malcolm reports that once he decided that the movement should have a newspaper, he located a printer and founded a paper which he named "Mr. Muhammad Speaks." That, of course, is not precisely what occurred. Shortly after the airing of "The Hate That Hate Produced," Malcolm came to my home in Queens and asked me if I would assist him in publishing a newspaper. He anguished for more than an hour over the fact that none of the members of his group had writing and editing skills; he argued that such trained black men as Carl Rowan, Ted Poston, and myself should forsake the white devils we worked for and contribute our talent and experience to Elijah. I was impressed by Malcolm's sincere desire to train young members of his group and readily agreed to help them write and edit the paper. I was torn between my deep disagreement with Malcolm's philosophy and my commitment to the notion that one should seize every opportunity to provide training-skills to young Negroes. But there was more. By then I had known Malcolm for about a year; I watched him grow and realized that I was having some influence on his thinking. The Malcolm of the pulpit was one man, but the private Malcolm was another; his thirst for knowledge was unquenchable, and he was the most voracious reader I have ever encountered. One afternoon I asked him if he had ever thought of the fact that the American race problem had overtones of class conflict: I then suggested that Oswald Spengler had written of this in *The Decline Of The West*, a book published in the early thirties. The following after-noon Malcolm came to my home bleary-eyed and bursting with ideas; he had withdrawn the complete Spengler from the library and stayed up all night reading.

Malcolm and several other members of the move-ment wrote the copy for the paper and I did the editing. I wrote some of the articles myself after Malcolm had given me the ideas he wished con-veyed. Then came another memorable moment; once we were ready to go to press, I had to shatter Malcolm with the news that there was not a Negro print shop in New York capable of turning out a newspaper.

"You mean we are going to have to let a devil print the paper?" he fired back. But even as he reacted, Malcolm was understanding an argument those of us who were his non-Muslim friends had been pressing: That even if we wanted to, the American Negro, at this juncture was in no position to undertake a "go it alone, separate state" venture.

I located a printer in Brooklyn, a Jew. He readily agreed to print the paper, saying, "I don't give a damn what Malcolm writes about white people, so long as he doesn't write anything bad about Jews!"

The press did roll, and the first several issues of the paper were called *The Islamic News*. It was later changed to *Mr. Muhammad Speaks*. Eric Lincoln notes in his book, that the paper reflected a "professional hand." Lincoln knew well whose hand

it was; on at least one occasion he helped Malcolm
and me correct galley proofs.

These matters assume importance because they
show how Malcolm seized the Black Muslim movement, and with a lusty assist from those of us who
respected him, while disagreeing with his dogma,
transmuted it into a something neither Elijah nor
Farad dreamt of.

Despite the fact that Malcolm began almost
every sentence by saying, "The Honorable Elijah
Muhammad teaches us that . . . ," the thousands who
heard him speaking were fascinated by Malcolm,
not by Elijah. The Malcolm who once spent his days
and nights "fishing" for lost black souls in Harlem
was now telling the "white devils" of Yale, Har-
vard, and Colgate of their impending doom at the
hands of the black man. And it was at Yale that one
white student cried out with guilt and jumped
from a balcony while Malcolm spoke.

As it had for Martin Luther King, the pulpit
became too narrow Malcolm X: Neither organization was big enough for the expanding and explod-
ing mind of either man.

SIX

THE HATE THAT HATE PRODUCED

Now that Malcolm has been assassinated and is being martyred, considerable debate rages over just what dogma, precisely, Malcolm was preaching in his early and raw years as Elijah's Minister. A number of scholars, black and white, have contacted me in search of the transcript of the telecast, "The Hate That Hate Produced." Because the telecast involved the first major news coverage of both Elijah Muhammad and Malcolm X, I have elected to print the entire section of the documentary dealing with the Black Muslim movement. Historians will be particularly interested in the degree to which the interviews prophesied the racial unrest that grips the nation today, almost ten years later:

* *

WALLACE: Good evening. I'm Mike Wallace. Last week on Newsbeat, our 5:30 news program here on Channel 13, we presented a five-part series, which we called "The Hate That Hate Produced," a study of the rise of Black Racism... of a call for Black Supremacy... among a small but growing segment of the American Negro population. Tonight, because of the considerable interest evoked by the serialized version, we are repeating this disturbing story with additional film sequences which we did not have time to use last week.

So, now, "The Hate That Hate Produced!"

While city officials, state agencies, white liberals
and sober-minded Negroes stand idly by, a group
of Negro dissenters is taking to street corner step-
ladders, church pulpits, sports arenas and ballroom platforms across the U.S., to preach a gospel
of hate that would set off a federal investigation if
it were preached by Southern Whites. What are they
saying? Listen ...

SPEAKER: "I charge the white man with being the
greatest liar on earth. I charge the white man with
being the greatest drunkard on earth. I charge the
white man with being the greatest swine-eater on
earth. Yet, the Bible forbids it. I charge the white
man with being the greatest gambler on earth. I
charge the white man, ladies and gentlemen of the
jury, with being the greatest murderer on earth. I
charge the white man with being the greatest
peace-breaker on earth. I charge the white man
with being the greatest adulterer on earth. I charge
the white man with being the greatest robber on
earth. I charge the white man with being the greatest deceiver on earth. I charge the white man with
being the greatest trouble-maker on earth. So therefore, ladies and gentlemen of the jury, I ask you,
bring back a verdict of guilty as charged."

WALLACE: The indictment you have just heard is
being delivered over and over again, in most of the
major cities across the country. This charge comes
at the climax of a morality play, called THE
TRIAL. The play, indeed the message of the play,
is that the white man has been put on trial for his
sins against the black man; he has been found guilty.
The sentence is *death* ... The play is sponsored and
produced by a Negro religious group who call
themselves the Muslims. They use a good deal of

the paraphernalia of the traditional religion of Islam, but they are fervently disavowed by orthodox Moslems. These home-grown Negro-American Muslims are the most powerful of the Black Supremacist groups. They now claim a membership of at least a quarter of a million Negroes. Their doctrine is being taught in 50 cities across the nation. Let no one underestimate the Muslims. They have their own parochial schools, like this one in Chicago, where Muslim children are taught to hate the white man. Even the clothes they wear are in sharp contrast to American dress ... like these two Negro children going to school. Wherever they go, the Muslims withdraw from the life of the community. They have their own stores, supermarkets, barbershops, restaurants. Here you see a progressive, modern, air-conditioned Muslim department store on Chicago's South Side. Their story of hatred for the white man is carried in many Negro newspapers. Here you see their Minister, Malcolm X, proudly displaying five of the biggest Negro papers in America ... papers published in Los Angeles, New York, Pittsburgh, Detroit and Newark. Negro politicians, regardless of their private belief, listen when the leaders of the Black Supremacist movement speak. Here you see Manhattan Borough President Hulan Jack shaking hands with Elijah Muhammad, the leader of the Muslims. And here you see City Councilman Earl Brown addressing a Muslim rally. Four or five times a year, the Muslims assemble in one of America's major cities to hear their leader, Elijah Muhammad. This coming Sunday afternoon they will gather in New York's St. Nicholas Arena to hear him. But, here you see them arriving at Washington's Uline Arena for a meeting they held just six weeks ago. Every devout Muslim is eager to attend these meetings for, some time between now and 1970, and at just such a rally as this, the Muslim leader has intimated he will give the call for the Destruction of the White Man. As you will see, every precaution is taken to protect their leader at these meetings. The Muslims, both men and women, submit to a complete search before they finally enter the meeting hall. Some ten thousand persons attended the rally you see here. All of them were searched. That's a search going on here ... this process began three hours before the meeting started. And shortly you will see Elijah Muhammad, founder and spiritual leader of the group. His flock is waiting for him now, and finally here comes their spiritual leader ... Elijah Muhammad. He is actually Elijah Poole of Hawkinsville, Georgia. During World War II, Muhammad was arrested and charged with sedition and draft-dodging; the Department of Justice finally dropped the charge that he had advocated defeat of the white democracies and victory for the "colored Japanese." But Muhammad and his followers did serve time in the federal penitentiary for refusing to register for the draft. Here you will hear Elijah Muhammad, introduced by Minister Malcolm X, the Muslim's New York leader and ambassador-at-large for the movement. The "good news" that Minister X talks about here is the coming rise of the black man and the fall of the white man.

MINISTER X: "Everyone who is here today realizes that we are now living in the fulfillment of prophesy. We have come to hear and to see the greatest and wisest and most fearless black man in America today. In the Church, we used to sing the song 'Good News, The Chariot is Coming,' is that right or wrong?"

AUDIENCE: "Right!"

MINISTER X: "But what we must bear in mind is that what's good news to one person is bad news to another. While you sit here today, knowing that you have come to hear good news, you must realize in advance, that what might be good news for you might be bad news for somebody else. What's good news for the sheep might be bad news for the wolves."

WALLACE: The "good news" for the black man is that he is on the verge of recapturing his position as Ruler of the Universe. The "bad news" for the white man is that his long and wicked reign will shortly be over. And following this introduction, Elijah Muhammad, leader of the Muslims, speaks:

MUHAMMAD: "The Christian religion has failed. Now the Government of America has failed you. You have no justice coming from no one. It is written that we are like sheep among wolves . . . every wolf taking a bite at you. You want justice. You want freedom. You want equality ... but get none."

WALLACE: Following this speech, which lasted some two hours, Newsbeat reporter Louis Lomax interviewed Elijah Muhammad, the spiritual leader of the Muslims ...

LOMAX: "Although you have said that the white race is doomed and that they are a race of devils, do you make any distinction—are there any good white people? For example, suppose I were to ask you whom you think was the best white man—is there any such thing?"

MUHAMMAD: "I'll let the Bible answer that. They say, no, not one is good."

LOMAX: "Now if I have understood your teachings correctly, you teach that all of the members of

Islam are God, and that one among you is supreme, and that that one is Allah. Now, have I understood you correctly?"

MUHAMMAD: "That's right."

LOMAX: "Now, you have on the other hand said, that Allah has taught you that the devil is the white man—that the white man is a doomed race."

MUHAMMAD: "Yes.".

LOMAX: "Now you have said, sir, that between now and approximately 1970 there should come a reawakening."

MUHAMMAD: "A general resurrection."

LOMAX: "Of the American Negro."

MUHAMMAD: "That's right."

LOMAX: "And that the extended time for the white man may well run out and that it will come in terms of war between God and the devil—this coming destruction of the white man. Will there be any bloodshed involved in this or will it be a completely mental thing?"

MUHAMMAD: "According to the teachings of the prophets of old, and of God himself, there will be plenty bloodshed . . . plenty of it."

LOMAX: "Have you ever been accused, sir, of preaching hate?"

MUHAMMAD: "Yes."

LOMAX: "Do you think you are?"

MUHAMMAD: "No."

LOMAX: "What are you preaching, sir?"

MUHAMMAD: "The truth."

LOMAX: "And if the truth is irritable, or . . ."

MUHAMMAD: ". . . classified as hate, then I cannot help that."

WALLACE: But of even more interest to New Yorkers is Malcolm X, the Muslims' New York minister . . . He is a remarkable man. A man who, by his own admission, was once a procurer and dope peddler. He served time for robbery in the Michigan and Massachusetts State Penitentiaries. But now he is a changed man. He will not smoke or drink. He will not even eat in a restaurant that houses a tavern. He told Newsbeat that his life changed for him when the Muslim faith taught him no longer to be ashamed to be a black man. Reporter Lomax asked Minister Malcolm X to further explain the Muslim teachings of Elijah Muhammad . . .

LOMAX: ". . . that in the same context that Mr. Elijah Muhammad teaches . . . that his faith . . . the Islamic faith is for the black man and that the black man is good. He also uses the Old Testament instance of the serpent in Adam and Eve and the Garden of Eden, and he sets up the proposition that this is the great battle between good and evil, and he uses the word devils."

MINISTER X: "Yes."

LOMAX: "He uses it almost interchangeably and synonymous with the word snake. Well, what does he mean there?"

MINISTER X: "Well, number one, he teaches us that there never was a real serpent."

LOMAX: "It was not a real serpent . . ."

MINISTER X: ". . . that went into the Garden."

LOMAX: "What was it?"

MINISTER X: "But as you know, the Bible was written in symbols and parables, and this serpent or snake is a symbol that's used to hide the real identity of the one whom that actually was."

LOMAX: "Well, who was it?"

MINISTER X: "The white man."

LOMAX: "I want to call your attention, Minister Malcolm, to one paragraph in this column. He says and I quote him, 'The only people born of Allah are the black nation, of whom the so-called American Negroes are descendants.'"

MINISTER X: "Yes."

LOMAX: "Now is this your standard teaching?"

MINISTER X: "Yes. He teaches us that the black man by nature is divine."

LOMAX: "Now, does this mean that the white man by nature is evil?"

MINISTER X: "By nature, he is other than divine."

LOMAX: "Well, now, does this mean he is evil? Can he do good?"

MINISTER X: "By nature he is evil."

LOMAX: "He cannot do good?"

MINISTER X: "History is best qualified to reward all research and we don't have any historic example where we have found that they collectively as a people have done good."

LOMAX: "Minister Malcolm, you now, in Chicago and in Detroit, have universities of Islam, do you not?"

MINISTER X: "Yes, sir, in Detroit and Chicago."

LOMAX: "And you take your parishioners ... you take children from the kindergarten ages and you train them right through high school, is that true?"

MINISTER X: "Yes, sir, from the age of four, I think, upward."

LOMAX: "And you have a certified parochial school operating in Chicago ..."

MINISTER X: "In Chicago ..."

LOMAX: "And in Detroit."

MINISTER X: "And in Detroit."

LOMAX: "And kids come to your school in lieu of going to what we would call regular day school?"

MINISTER X: "Yes, sir, many."

LOMAX: "What do you teach them there?"

MINISTER X: "We teach them the same things that they would be taught ordinarily in school, minus the Little Black Sambo story and the things that were taught to you and me when we were coming up to breed that inferiority complex in us."

LOMAX: "Do you teach them what you have just said to me—that the white man is the symbol of evil?"

MINISTER X: "You can go to any little Muslim child and ask them where is hell or who is the devil, and he wouldn't tell you that hell is down in the ground or that the devil is something invisible that you can't see. He'll tell you that hell is right where he has been catching it and he'll tell you the one who is responsible for him having received this hell is the devil."

LOMAX: "And he would say that this devil is the white man?"

MINISTER X: "Yes."

LOMAX: "Can a white man join your temple?"

MINISTER X: "None has ever joined."

LOMAX: "If one came up and attempted to join would he be allowed to come in and be taught?"

MINISTER X: "No, sir."

LOMAX: "Why not?"

MINISTER X: "Well, that's one of the reasons why most people think that Mr. Muhammad teaches hate but if there is a rattlesnake in the field who has been biting your brothers and your sisters, then you go and tell them that that's a rattlesnake and all of the harm that's ever come to them has come to them from that particular source. Well, then that rattler will think that the warner is teaching hate. He'll go back and tell the other snakes that this man is teaching hate ... this man is teaching hate ... but it's not hate ... it's just that when you study people who have been harmed and discover the source of their injury—the source of all of their defects, and you begin to point out that source, it's not that you hate the source, but your love for your people is so intense—so great—that you must let them know what is wrong with them, what is the cause of their ills. And this is one of the basic factors, I believe, involved, when the propaganda is put out that Mr. Muhammad teaches hate. He teaches black people to love each other, and our love for each other is so strong, we don't have any room left in our hearts."

LOMAX: "What do you think of the NAACP?"

MINISTER X: "Islam is a natural religion, and it is difficult to find a black body with a white head and classify that body as something natural. Most organizations that represent the so-called Negro, usually we find when we study them that though they are supposed to be for us, the leadership or the brain-power or the political power or whatever power that runs it usually is the white man."

WALLACE: We have, thus, seen Muslim leaders in reflective moments and as they talk to members of their own flock. But what about their approach to non-Muslim Negroes? Three months ago Minister Malcolm X was invited to speak at a Harlem rally, celebrating African Freedom Day. His audience was composed chiefly of Christian Negroes, with a lively interest in African affairs. We have obtained filmed segments of that speech. The film was made under adverse circumstances, but you will be able to hear and understand Minister Malcolm X, as he addresses a non-Muslim audience.

MINISTER X: "Who is his enemy? He'll say the Belgian. Ask the man in Kenya who is his enemy, he'll say the British. Ask the man in Morocco who is his enemy, he'll say the French. But the one thing that the French and the British and the Belgians all have in common—they're all from Europe. How could so few white people rule so many black people. This is the thing you should want to know. How could so few? The white man today will tell you that thousands of years ago the black man in Africa was living in palaces, the black man in Africa was wearing silk, the black man in Africa was cooking and seasoning his food, the black man in Africa has mastered the arts and the sciences ... he knew the course of the stars and the universe before the man up in Europe knew that the earth wasn't flat. Is that right or wrong? Then, if the black man in Africa had reached such a high state of civilization so long ago, at a time when the people of Europe were crawling on their all fours, what happened to make these people or enable these people to come out of the caves and come down into our civilization and take it over and hitch us to the plow—what happened? How did they do it? These are the things you should want to find out before you say hurray, hurray, hurray. Is that right or wrong?"

AUDIENCE: "You are right!"

* *

The telecast laid bare once and for all the racial ferment that rumbled unseen and unheard beneath New York's façade of good race relations. Mike Wallace himself was visibly moved—almost to tears, actually—as he concluded the documentary with these words:

WALLACE: It is a terrible indictment of America that even a small part of our Negro population—

even a small part—is willing to pay heed to the racist declarations we have heard here tonight.

For them, and for all Negroes, we must make America live up to the fine language of our creed. We must make ourselves in reality a nation of one people, indivisible, with freedom and justice for all. In such a nation there would be no place for the white supremacists who disgrace and embitter our society today. And in such a nation there would have been no occasion to report the melancholy story of "The Hate That Hate Produced." Mike Wallace ... Good night.

SEVEN

INTEGRATION

The issue of "integration" provided the essential conflict between Malcolm X and Martin Luther King; the issue lives on, after their deaths, and is the crucial explanation for their martyrdom by different groups advocating dissimilar racial philosophies.

At the core, here, is the complex question of just how, precisely, is the black man to define his existence in America? Historically the Negro has progressed from indentured servitude into chattel slavery, then into a segregated status and, finally, into the current era that can only be described as "integration"—at least, to some extent. Yet the story is a bit more tortured than that. During the latter 1800's, many white Christians began to feel that the only moral way out was to return Negro slaves to Africa. The country of Liberia was founded for just this purpose but comparatively few Negroes migrated there. This was a historical point Malcolm would have done well to ponder. As miserable as things were for black Americans during slavery, the records show that free black men opposed the "African colonization" program and refused to leave what they considered their homeland. It is significant that such men as Henry Clay and John Randolph favored the plan and were beaten back by such Negro leaders as Richard Allen, the founder of the African Methodist Episcopal

Church. Allen provides a clue as to what had happened: Refused permission to worship fully in segregated whites' churches, Negroes had formed their own religious organizations. Clearly, then, Negro institutional life had begun to take root, and with the American imprimatur at that. The plan of returning to Africa was rendered moot once slavery ended, and the assumption then was that the Negro would occupy a separate but parallel society in America. This was the kind of society early Negro professionals were willing to accept, and it may well have worked had the black and white societies been truly equal, and had white men not turned the Negro society into an enclave of terror and brutality. It will be recalled that even Martin Luther King, Jr. was willing, initially, to settle the Montgomery bus issue on grounds based on segregation. And it is also a historical fact that the Supreme Court had ordered segregated schools after Southern boards of education refused to comply with an "equal but separate" order.

Even so, integration was already the pattern of life in the North, and it is my own view that the overwhelming perplexity of American life would have forced the practice upon the South. As the main body of black leadership was moving toward integration, a small band of Negroes still pressed for emigration to Africa, and it was they who organized around Marcus Garvey. Malcolm's father was a devout Garveyite, and Malcolm was never able to overcome that influence. More than any other man, Malcolm forged the fuzzy rhetoric that engulfed the issue; he confused "integration" with "assimilation" and then went on to exhort Negroes to preserve their Arabic culture and language, something they never had. Malcolm's main thrust was theological, the teaching that the wicked "white devil" was to be destroyed and that the black man would be destroyed with him unless he separated. This separation was to be both geographical and spiritual. As a matter of fact, according to Elijah and Malcolm, the white man's time expired shortly before the first world war. God, Allah, had spared the white man in order to give Negroes time to escape to a separate nation. During the first year of my friendship with Malcolm, he seemed uncertain as to just where the black nation should be located; then one day he raced into the printing plant and ordered me to prepare a headline, "We Must Have Land Of Our Own." That was the first mention I had heard of the idea of separate states here in America. I immediately offered him Mississippi; he refused it.

Malcolm's aggressive and vitriolic attack against integration led him to publicly excoriate the black leaders of the civil rights movement. He called the NAACP a "freak" because it was "a black body with a white head," and he accused the United Nation's Undersecretary, Dr. Ralph Bunche, of selling out the Arabs to the Jews. In one outburst, Malcolm called Roy Wilkins, the Executive Secretary of the NAACP, a "judas," and referred to Martin Luther King as "Reverend Dr. Chickenwing," an obvious reference to the Southern legend that black ministers fancy fried chicken.

Malcolm's scabrous attack came at a time when the civil rights movement could least afford it. King's success at Montgomery had led to the formation of the Southern Christian Leadership Council, a new civil rights organization that in turn played midwife to the Student Nonviolent Coordinating Committee. With both the NAACP and the Urban

League sidelined, King, the young college students, and CORE usurped the center stage and carried out street demonstrations that yielded historic results. Relationships between the various civil rights organizations were, to put it mildly, strained and there was a year-long period during which it seemed that open conflict would occur between the various leaders. Not only was Malcolm's attack disturbing to the already embattled Negro leadership, but his separatist gospel played into the hands of those white groups who bitterly opposed any move toward integration. During several public debates with Malcolm, I was astonished that white students enjoyed being called "snakes and devils" by a black man who then went on to advocate separation of the races. Several of us had tried for years to validate or disprove the report that Malcolm received considerable financial support from H. L. Hunt and other conservative forces in the South. Our efforts failed.

The white South made it increasingly difficult to counter Malcolm. There were the dogs and the fire hoses at Birmingham and Selma; then Malcolm could say, "Any man who will sick four-legged dogs on black women and children is a two-legged dog!" There were the white riots at Southern schools; then Malcolm could say, "Only a fool would want to integrate with people who throw bricks at little black school children!" The now famous "March On Washington" proved Malcolm was an excellent marksman.

Negro leaders, specifically Martin Luther King and Roy Wilkins, were at bitter odds over whether the event should be staged. King carried the day, and then Wilkins joined in. Once it was clear that the march would take place, President John F.

Kennedy ordered all liquor stores and bars in Washington closed, and so stationed the Washington police and the army that we literally marched into an armed camp. Malcolm charged that white leaders, from church and labor groups, moved in and controlled the march; he was right. Malcolm charged that the speech delivered by John Lewis, the President of SNCC, was censored because it contained remarks the Catholic Bishop of Washington felt were inflamatory and revolutionary; he was right. Several days after the march, there was major racial bloodshed in Mississippi, and Malcolm could shout, "Martin Luther King's dream is now a nightmare!"

Had Malcolm relegated his attack to "integration" and certain civil rights leaders alone, he might have escaped relatively unscathed. But when he broadened his offensive to include the Christian church, particularly the black Christian church, he swam into turbulent and troubled waters. But Malcolm was spoiling for a fight, a public wrangle, and he opened the issue with this sermon:

"In the past, the 'religious roads' leading through black America presented smooth sailing for the 'Old Touring Cars' (churches) of Christianity. They met few obstacles and had little opposition or competition. The 'drivers' (preachers) had it easy. Their 'course' was never challenged. They ruled supreme on the religious roads of black America.

"However, today, time is making a great CHANGE. The religious roads of black America have suddenly become blocked by a ROCKY BARRIER, and all the black and white preachers combined are incapable of removing it. The firm, down-to-earth, thought-provoking teachings of the religion of Islam are now obstructing this path over

which it was once easy sailing for these preachers
of white man's Christianity.

"Islam poses both a challenge and a threat because Islam is the 'resurrecting power.' Thousands
of so-called Negroes are beginning for the first time
to think for themselves, since turning away from
the segregated Christian church, and are rejoining
the ranks of their black brothers and sisters of the
East. Their age-old faith is the religion of Islam, the
religion of our foreparents, the true religion of
black mankind.

"The same slave master's Christian religion promised us that we (Negroes) would sprout wings
after death and fly up into the sky where God
would have a place especially prepared for us.

"Since we poor 'cursed' slaves were not to get
anything on earth while we were alive, we soon
learned to expect it only after death, 'up in the sky.'
Thus, this earth, and all its vast riches which we
ourselves originally owned, was left to the deceitful
maneuverings of the white race, for them to build a
heaven for themselves and their own kind, 'in THIS
life.'

"Such religious teachings were purposely designed to make us (so-called Negroes) feel inferior
to the white Christian slave master. Soon he was
successful in making us fear him, obey him, and
worship him ... instead of the true Supreme Being,
the God of our own foreparents, Almighty God,
ALLAH."

Even Malcolm was stunned at the rejoinders.
Black clergymen took to their pulpits, to both the
radio and television media, to denounce Malcolm
and his gospel as purveyors of hate, untruth and
despair. The Negro press entered the controversy
and Malcolm never was able to unfasten the badge

of hate that was pinned on him during the exchange. He was later to regret this intemperate moment but at that time he was man obsessed by his own aggressiveness. A few days later he shocked the nation with a television statement in which he said God had slapped down a chartered plane loaded with white people from Atlanta, Georgia, as retribution for two Black Muslims who had been killed during a gun battle with police in Los Angeles. Even Elijah took umbrage at this statement and Malcolm was called in and given the first of several warnings.

Integration, which for most of us meant nothing more than total equality of education and opportunity, was on the increase, but something was wrong. Malcolm's popularity was increasing geometrically, and despite his splendid work in the South, Martin Luther King was growing unpopular in the North. His intemperate remarks aside, Malcolm had properly isolated his audience: The black ghetto poor of the North to whom "integration" made no sense whatsoever. For a while the battle for integration had been raging in the courts, and in the streets the big city ghetto had spawned a generation of disillusioned black men who had neither stakes in nor love for American society as it is now constituted.

"The ghetto is on the verge of a bloody explosion," Malcolm warned. Several days later Martin Luther King made this comment to a newsman:

"Unless the race issue is soon resolved, this nation will experience the kind of violence that is unparalleled in modern history."

This is one of the few times the two men approached agreement.

EIGHT

VIOLENCE

Now it is Martin Luther King, Jr. who brings the issue to the fore.

American race relations have always been flecked by violence. Slavery was maintained through brute force, free blacks rioted in the North sporadically throughout the 19th century, and white night riders made the words "flogging" and "lynching" part of the American lexicon. The possibility that Negroes would resort to violence has always lain near the surface of American thought and even the NAACP was hard pressed to convince some whites that upon its founding it would not become a black Ku Klux Klan.

Not only is violence a part of the American tradition it is endemic to the human tradition as well. Man has almost always solved his conflicts violently and there is not a single group, racial or religious, that has not employed violence as a method of achieving its goals. Lyndon Johnson—speaking of Viet Nam, of course—is not the first American president to tell the nation "we must back our resolve with steel." The assumption was that the Negro would defy history and refuse to take up arms against the white man. Had he fulfilled this hope the black man would have been unique indeed. And Martin Luther King was forced to announce "nonviolence" because he was taking the protest movement out of the courtrooms and conference chambers into the streets. This meant that ordinary blacks and whites would be put in direct confrontation and thus the possibility of mutual violence was increased.

King was deeply influenced by the works of Gandhi, Thoreau, and, of course, Jesus. I am convinced that he felt that nonviolence was the Negro's best tactical weapon; I am also convinced that he had a deep moral commitment to nonviolence, to the notion that he who lives by the sword shall die by the sword. Martin was convinced that this weary and troubled world of ours was capable of forging plowshares and studying war no more. And he believed that practical and significant changes could be brought about through nonviolence. The core of his nonviolent philosophy, then, was his assumption that white people were men of conscience and that once nonviolently confronted they would share their power and position.

The operative phrase in Martin's philosophy was "creative tension." The concept is not as nonviolent as many people supposed. It meant that once you are certain as to the justness of your cause you must march thousands of unarmed bodies into the hostile community, defy the local law, and create tension between the marchers and the "oppressors." The purpose was to fill his jails and challenge his mores to the point where he behaves violently; once the oppressor resorts to violence the marchers refuse to retaliate or even defend themselves. They curl up, fetuslike, and take it. It is at this point, according to Martin Luther King, that enraged world opinion takes form and demands basic social changes. Thus it was that men like Sheriffs Bull Connor and Jim Clarke became natural foils for Martin. He could always depend on them to gas and dog-chase enough blacks, along with their white supporters, to get revolutionary laws through Congress. The tactic worked in Birmingham, Montgomery, Selma, and in a score of cities in the South.

This is why it must be said that, but for television, neither Martin King nor his tactic would have succeeded. The horrible events of Birmingham and Selma shocked millions of white people who never had eyewitnessed the brutal nature of the problem. And then Martin received an unexpected assist from the individual whites who bombed churches and buried slain civil rights workers under bridges.

Martin King appeared on the civil rights scene at a time when it was becoming clear that the white South was not going to obey the Supreme Court's desegregation orders. The decade beginning in 1954 saw the most massive defiance of law in our history, certainly since the Civil War. The South's reply to these orders was "Never!" And it was this defiance that rendered the NAACP impotent and gave King his arena. The American Negro faced two choices: Either he would acquiesce in the South's defiance or he would have to take up arms. Martin provided the third alternative: A nonviolent, tension-creating confrontation with those who were in defiance of law and justice. But for his leadership, his channeling of the frustration and anger of blacks, the republic would have erupted with riots several years before Watts. His detractors went into action the day the Montgomery bus boycott started and they are persisting through these early days of his martyrdom.

Let me make short work of Martin's white detractors who charged him with being a communist, or communist dupe, as well as those who rested their arguments on strong segregationist convictions. As to the charge of communism, Martin made it abundantly clear that he was not a communist. Only an anti-communist zealot would urge such a charge in the face of Martin's deep commitment to the Christian proposition. But the same Christian commitment led him to believe that free men have the right to embrace communism if they wish; he also felt they had the right to work in the civil rights movement. During the years of his leadership he admitted more than one communist to his staff, much to the chagrin of some of his close associates. As for the segregationalists they deserve little attention here; they opposed all change, many of them felt slavery was the just way of things, and they felt that any Negro who marched, including Stepin Fetchet, was an *uppity nigger* and a radical.

But a considerable segment of the white population that was not necessarily segregationalist became highly critical of Martin King. Their effective epithet was "troublemaker"; the charge was that wherever he went Martin produced trouble, that although he was for nonviolence there was always violence wherever he marched. Martin's reply, and mine, was that he was simply trying to make social reality out of the laws of both man and God as he understood them; the trouble was created by white people who were determined to deny black men justice and the violence was the act of white men and Martin's detractors, never the deeds of Martin's followers. This includes the violence that occurred in the midst of Martin's last march in Memphis which I shall deal with in a later chapter.

I discussed these critics with Martin on many occasions and I know they troubled him deeply. They troubled him because they italicized a practical flaw in his nonviolent philosophy. He had assumed that the average white American who was simply indifferent to the race issue would see the justness, the morality, of Martin's cause and then proceed to the theological-philosophical conclusion that the just man has a moral duty to challenge injustice regardless of what hell-raising the unjust would consequently engender. Martin felt that the just man's insistence upon justice would produce change. Are Africans who demanded independence morally to blame for the British reign of terror in Kenya, the French violence in Algieria, and Belgian terror in the Congo? And are this nation's founding fathers to be morally blamed for the Revolutionary War? It was Martin's total conviction that those demanding independence were just men, that had independence been granted there would have been no bloodshed, and that the bloodshed was the doing of the oppressor, not the just men.

But there were two factors Martin King over- looked. The first was that white steelworkers in Gary, Indiana, are not seminary graduates; they are law-and-order advocates because this, in their view, is the guardian of their property and families. And when they see violence in the streets, they condemn the leader of the march, regardless of his cause, not those who react violently to the march. In short, the average white American is the kind of fellow who does not care what happens so long as it does not disturb or threaten him. But if the Bill of Rights was submitted to a referendum in Mississippi it would be overwhelmingly defeated, and if Jesus went to Cicero, Illinois, and took on the money- lenders he would suffer a crucifixion more brutal than the one carried out by the Romans.

The second factor Martin overlooked—perhaps he did see it—was best evidenced in Kenya. In that African country, the blacks tired of begging for independence from Britain and organized something called the Mau Mau; the group killed scores of white people and their ultimate goal was the annihilation of all British. They stopped short of that mainly because Kenya got her independence and Jomo Kenyatta, the leader of the group is now Premier of Kenya.

Martin King's second major source of criticism came from Malcolm X. It was far more serious and devastating. Once again Malcolm used his eloquence to pervert words. In a brilliant, but mean, maneuver Malcolm took to the streets of Harlem and made "nonviolence" the antithesis of "self-defense." Thus, he could mount a street corner platform in Harlem at the very moment Negro demonstrators were being kicked and beaten in Birmingham and say, "The Honorable Elijah Muhammad teaches us to defend ourselves and our families. If a blue-eyed devil hits you, your only recourse is to make sure you outlive him!"

"Yes, yes, yes," the crowd shouted back.

The perversion, as Malcolm well knew, was in the fact that we were demonstrating in Birmingham as a group, and under a tactical plan that called for nonviolence. But the manner in which Malcolm pressed his point gave the impression that Martin King was telling individual Negroes to allow white people to brutalize them individually and in their homes without mounting a defense. That was not true. Indeed, I once asked Martin during a television interview what he would do if someone, white or black, entered his home and menaced his wife and children. He replied, "Louis, I don't know what I would do; my advocacy of nonviolence is as a tactic during demonstrations, not as a total private way of life."

Malcolm X clearly understood this, but he also realized that the blacks in the northern ghetto were a captive audience. They were in no mood to hear preachments about loving white people and nonviolence. Even then the young blacks were in the mood to burn America down, and Malcolm well knew it. Martin also realized that the black Zeitgeist had gotten ahead of him. How strange that the spirit of the times, that of 1960, having overtaken the NAACP's legalistic approach to racial difficulty, had now outrun Martin King's concept of nonviolence. Not even Malcolm advocated aggressive violence, yet violence was in the air. It was just a matter of time.

NINE

MALCOLM VERSUS THE ORGANIZATION

Although their respective pulpits had become much, much, too narrow for both men, both Martin Luther King, Jr. and Malcolm X remained on their respective platforms in order to guarantee themselves a hearing—Malcolm did this even more so than Martin did.

Malcolm claims that he increased the membership in the Black Muslim movement from about four thousand to approximately forty thousand. It would be difficult indeed to dispute these figures. Malcolm rose in a matter of five years from the Assistant Ministership of Temple Number Two in Detroit to Minister of Temple Number Seven in New York, and he was by then Elijah Muhammad's roving minister-evangelist as well. The record shows that Malcolm was responsible for the proliferation of temples (they were later renamed "mosques") all along the East Coast, from Washington, D.C. to New England. In the beginning, as I have already noted, Malcolm's mission was to convert the "deaf, dumb, and blind black men" lost in the wilderness of North America to the teachings of The Honorable Elijah Muhammad. But whereas Elijah's gospel had been primarily geared to the salvation of the black man for more than thirty years, Malcolm by sheer dent of his personality and eloquence transmuted this gospel into a broadside attack on Negro leadership, something Elijah had never done with such vigor. And it was this platform maneuver that gave Malcolm such a large hearing at the nation's predominantly white universities.

Similarly, Martin Luther King found it imperative to project a wider gospel while, essentially, remaining on the same platform. He resigned his pastorate of the Dexter Avenue Baptist Church in Montgomery and returned to Atlanta, where he once again became his father's co-pastor at Ebenezer. More significantly Martin devoted most of his time to his post as Executive Director of the Southern Christian Leadership Council. Martin surrounded himself with black clergymen and, although his gospel and actions were to be wide ranging, this riveted him and his organization to a Christian base from which he could not have escaped even if he had wished to. There were those who then—and now—questioned whether this was not too restrictive a base for a man of Martin's dimensions; this was a cause of deep concern, and the concern was deepened by the fact that the overwhelming majority of Martin's advisers and confidants were black Baptists. It must be remembered that black Methodists have a major influence in the religious South, and that they and the Baptists have a long tradition of dislike and rivalry. The fear was that Martin would not be able to get the support of the Methodists that his movement deserved. On the whole, this fear proved to be justified. But not only did Martin endure, he prevailed. And his subsequent activity went a long way toward healing the breach between the black Methodists and Baptists. Indeed, his essentially Christian base was to later make it possible for Christians of all sects, black and white, to join his movement. There was never any doubt of Martin's belief in the basic tenents of the Christian propositions on which he stood.

The question of Malcolm's sincerity is another matter, and Malcolm created this doubt by publicly preaching dogmas many of us knew that he privately did not believe. As I will shortly prove, Malcolm persisted in this behavior until the day of his death. Knowing Malcolm as I did, I do not join those who often assailed him as being a hypocrite; rather I see his duplicity as that of a man who attempted to accomplish a certain goal while clinging to the only base at his disposal, a base he knew to be partially spurious.

The first evidence of this was Malcolm's gleeful preaching of Elijah's notions that white people are "devils." Since all black men are good and their religion is Islam, according to Elijah, then it follows that no white man can be a true Moslem. Malcolm preached this line thousands of times; each time he did it he knew it was false.

During the preparation of "The Hate That Hate Produced," Mike Wallace and I talked with spokesmen for the orthodox Islamic religion in New York. They did not excoriate Malcolm and the Black Muslims, but they made it clear that Islam was made up of, and welcomed, worshippers of all races. I confronted Malcolm with this and he maintained a stony silence.

Subsequently, Malcolm and I appeared on a late evening television program in Los Angeles. Malcolm was accompanied to the studio by John Shabazz, then the Captain of the Fruit of Islam in the Los Angeles Mosque. As we emerged from the studio to enter Brother John's car a number of Arab students from UCLA literally surrounded Malcolm.

They had seen the program and were visibly angered by Malcolm's "white devil" utterances. The students were as white as any white man, they were Moslems all, and they flatly accused Malcolm of preaching a false doctrine. Malcolm attempted to counter by saying that it was necessary for him to take the "white devil" approach in order to "wake up the deaf, dumb, and blind American Negro." The students would have none of Malcolm's defense and he stalked away from the group and entered the car. I have often wondered what he and Brother John talked about later that night.

These confrontations aside, can it honestly be assumed that so voracious a reader as Malcolm never paused to read the history of the faith he espoused? Had he done so, and he did, he would have discovered that Islam is, perhaps, the most open of all faiths when it comes to the questions of race and color. Can it be honestly assumed that Malcolm never pondered why orthodox followers of Islam who have lived in New York for years never worshipped at his Mosque? Are scholars to believe that it never occurred to Malcolm to visit and talk with members of Arabic delegations to the United Nations in New York?

Nor is this all:

(A) During the filming of "The Hate That Hate Produced," The Federation of Islamic Associations of Chicago, the official Moslem organization in the United States and Canada, denounced the Black Muslims as "teachers of race hatred."

It was the early and fiery Malcolm who struck back. He held these Moslems up to high ridicule, and then went on to say "they look very much like the blue-eyed devil who enslaved us and took away our culture." Malcolm went further and denounced these Moslems as "Europeans who passed us by in an attempt to make our slave masters Moslems!"

(B) In his autobiography, Malcolm gives a highly self-serving account of his holy journey to Mecca in 1965. Malcolm creates a "Paulinian moment" for himself, and the reader is entranced as Malcolm sees white Moslems and the scales fall from his eyes. The scene is climaxed during a personal audience with King Faisal of Saudi Arabia who bluntly tells Malcolm that he has been preaching "the wrong Islam."

Scholars will find this an astonishing moment indeed. After all—and he carefully omits this from his autobiography—Malcolm visited Egypt and other Arab countries several months before I did, in 1960. It was the holy season; Malcolm saw thousands of "white" Moslems enroute to Mecca. Malcolm had been given permission to make the journey to Mecca but deferred in order to let Elijah make the journey first, and thus give authenticity to the Black Muslim movement. This is why Malcolm could utter a firm "I know" when I told him I saw "white" Moslems in Africa. Subsequent to that I attended a Black Muslim rally at the Audubon Ballroom where Malcolm told Elijah's followers that he, Malcolm, had encountered Nasser while in Egypt; he said "Nasser looked just like you and me, a black man whom I wanted to embrace." Anyone who has seen Nasser's picture knows that is not true. But Malcolm went on to introduce the main speaker of the day, Akbar Muhammad, Elijah's son who had been studying at an Islamic University in Cairo for several years. Certainly Akbar knew the crude fallacy of the "white devil" teaching. The following year Elijah made the journey to Mecca.

And Elijah is far from color blind. The "white devil" teaching continued.

The only explanation for this, if one is to maintain faith in Malcolm's basic integrity, is that he carried out these public deceptions in order to maintain his organizational base. Had Malcolm and Elijah taught the truth about "integrated" Islam, the entire Black Muslim organizational structure would have collapsed; and, as later events were to prove conclusively, Malcolm would have had no place of retreat. But the "white devil" teaching was not the only duplicity Malcolm embraced to maintain his platform.

Elijah Muhammad's doctrine clearly predicts an ultimate conflict between God and the devil, that is to say, between the black man and the white man; and the black man will win, violently so. The doctrine also teaches black men to defend themselves and to take revenge if one of their number is brutalized by white men. This is the way Malcolm taught it:

"If a snake enters your home and bites your child you will take your shotgun and go looking for the snake. Now, if you come upon a snake you don't stop and examine his teeth to see if that is *the* snake who bit our child; they are all snakes and you shoot the snake you find!"

This always brought the black crowds to their feet with shouts of approval and the implicatio~ was unmistakable: If a white man brutalizes a black man then black men should go out and take revenge upon the first "snake" they come upon.

Then, in 1962, several Black Muslims became embroiled in a gun battle with Los Angeles police; one Black Muslim was killed, fourteen were wounded and arrested. The general black community reaction was that the police had launched an unwarranted attack on the Black Muslims and the entire matter climaxed with Malcolm X joining black Christian ministers in an unprecedented unity rally which roundly condemned the Los Angeles Police Department. The Black Muslims were itching for action, for revenge. Malcolm flew in from New York to give direction to the retaliation attack and only a last minute fiat from Elijah stopped them from carrying out what would have been a bloody act of retribution. Malcolm was stunned that Elijah stayed the Black Muslim's hand and it was a major task for even the eloquent Malcolm to explain to the Black Muslims why Elijah had stopped them from ferreting out the "snake" that had bitten their brethren. Malcolm was later to tell me that Elijah, to use a Southern expression, was "all breath and no britches," that Muhammad did not have the guts to back his gospel with steel.

This finally became a major irritant in Malcolm's side. After all Martin Luther King and others had black men in the streets across the nation demonstrating and facing personal harm. Malcolm, on the other hand, was calling white people "devils and snakes" but he wasn't doing anything. His promise that when the word is given the black man would destroy the white man was just as pie-in-the-skyish as the traditional religious notion that black men, along with others, would live on milk and honey in heaven in the great by-and-by. Malcolm began to smart under charges from militant blacks that he and his group were all talk and no action.

The matter was compounded by mounting reports that the Black Muslims were becoming fratricidal. There was some evidence that defectors from the movement had been physically assaulted; and there were veiled threats against well known Negro leaders. I now know that I was once marked for assassination; in June of 1968 John Shabass of New York (not to be confused with John Shabazz of Los Angeles) flatly told me he was among those assigned the "contract" against my life in 1962 and that he aborted the effort.

It is not even now clear who authorized violent acts against those black men who spoke against the Muslims. But violence was in the air. The feeling in the black community was best expressed by a black nationalist street corner orator in Harlem when he said "those damn Muslims are too scared to do anything to a white man; all they do is talk and beat up on other niggers!"

I remember a day in 1963, when James Farmer and I, along with hundreds of CORE members, carried out a demonstration against the building of an annex to Harlem Hospital by contractors who refused to hire Negro workers. As the confrontation moved to a showdown between the police and us, Malcolm and several hundred other blacks stood across the street watching.

"Watch yourself," Malcolm shouted at me. "Somebody is going to want to get some action. There is going to be trouble!"

"Trouble, hell!" I shouted back. "Quit talking and put your life on the line with us."

The tension was high, and even as I said it I realized that I had cut Malcolm badly. Hundreds of people applauded what I had said and it was a furious and reddening Malcolm that stalked away from the scene. We won the day without bloodshed or jailings. What I did not know was that Malcolm was consistently pressing Elijah Muhammad for permission to become involved in demonstrations.

Each time Malcolm received a flat and unequivocal "No!" It finally came to the point that Elijah ordered Malcolm not to raise the matter again. Malcolm obeyed.

On the day every television network carried scenes of Birmingham police dogs attacking black children, Malcolm went on camera to say, "Martin Luther King is a chump, not a champ; any man who puts his women and children on the front lines is a chump, not a champ." But what is to be said of a leader who does not field troops at all? This, in essence, was the storm cloud of doubt that was settling over Malcolm and the Black Muslim movement.

Again the record shows Malcolm's public duplicity. During his speech at New York's Audubon Ballroom, Akbar Muhammad did not correct the "white devil" teaching of his father but he did take Malcolm to the woodshed with several hundred people looking on:

"We must have unity among Negroes," Akbar said. "It is time for all of us—CORE, the NAACP, Dr. Martin Luther King, the Student Nonviolent Coordinating Committee, and the Black Muslim— to sit down together behind closed doors and unite. Negro leaders must now stop calling each other names. We must stop calling Dr. King names, and he must stop talking about us before the enemy. We may not be able to walk all the way to freedom together, but we can walk half the way together, so let's unite and walk together as far as we can."

But Malcolm was not phased; while the crowd was still applauding Akbar, Malcolm jumped to his feet to utter this stirring mea culpa and plea for financial help.

"I am guilty!" Malcolm told the crowd after

Akbar finished. "I am guilty of calling other Negro leaders names. As you know, no one had done more of that recently than I have. But today we have heard a new teaching, and we are all going to abide by it. . . . Now brothers with the white buckets will pass among you. And you integrate those white buckets with some green dollar bills. Meanwhile I am going to talk to you. . . . If you help Mr. Muhammad, you are helping the man who has helped you. The Honorable Elijah Muhammad is the man who has told you the truth about yourself; The Honorable Elijah Muhammad is the man who has told you the truth about the white man ... The Honorable Elijah Muhammad is the man who has made it possible for Brother Akbar to go to school back home in Egypt; The Honorable Elijah Muhammad is the man who tells you to look up; The Honorable Elijah Muhammad is the man who tells you to clean yourself up, provide for your wife and children, protect your family. The Honorable Elijah Muhammad will make you be true to your family; The Honorable Elijah Muhammad will get that monkey (dope addiction) off your back; The Honorable Elijah Muhammad will get this white, blue-eyed gorilla off your back!"

"Make it plain, Brother Minister, make it plain."

And it was in the name of "The Honorable Elijah Muhammad" that Malcolm was to carry out his final act of public duplicity in order to maintain his organizational base. For years it had been openly discussed that several of Elijah's private secretaries had been exiled from the movement after becoming pregnant; they were charged with adultery. The consensus among Negroes, Muslim and non-Muslim, was that Elijah had fathered the children. Malcolm admits in his autobiography that he had heard the rumors but that his faith in Elijah was of such caliber that he refused to harbor such notions. The reports mounted and so disturbed Malcolm that he searched out the exiled young women and received confirmation of all that had been said. It is then that Malcolm closeted with Elijah's son, who not only reconfirmed the indiscretions of his father, but warned Malcolm that Mr. Muhammad would not welcome any effort to explain away the adulterous acts. Even so Malcolm researched into both the Old and New Testaments to find passages that would justify a leader's private indiscretions on the basis that "a man's teaching is more important than his private deeds." Malcolm writes that he confronted Elijah with his findings, and that Elijah replied that these acts of sex with the young women had been carried out in "fulfillment of prophecy," that they were things that Elijah had to live out because he was of the same line as David and other prophets of God who had become involved in adultery. Malcolm, a deeply moral man concerning such matters, once again buckled. He went forth and prepared his fellow Black Muslim ministers to preach "the fulfillment of prophecy."

It is no demeaning of Malcolm X, then, to point out that he consistently preached a gospel he knew was riddled with untruths, and that he propped up an organization whose leader was in violation of his own moral doctrine. And as he did it, Malcolm well knew that he was betraying the thousands of Black Muslims who had been taxed with tithes and publicly punished because they had lapsed into such indiscretions as family fights and adultery.

Why did Malcolm do it? I think the answer lies in an angry statement Malcolm later made to Alex Haley, his biographer: "We had the best organization black men ever had and these niggers (his Black Muslim critics) ruined it."

A clear reading of Malcolm indicates that his every hope was to someday, somehow, purify the Black Muslim organization. Once Malcolm confirmed Elijah's adultery, he alerted his fellow ministers to keep Muhammad and his moral teaching in the background and to begin preaching about the political and economic salvation of the American black man. This would have led, in time, to a "Malcolmized" Black Muslim organization. But it was then that, with an assist from Malcolm himself, the men around Elijah jerked Malcolm's pulpit from beneath him.

Several organizational intrigues led to Malcolm's final break with Elijah Muhammad. Many of the strong men around Muhammad clearly understood that the organization would be "Malcolmized" if the fiery minister continued to dominate the headlines. As the organization's evangelist Malcolm was always on the go, taking the gospel to black and white audiences alike. But such men as John Ali were in Chicago with Elijah Muhammad; they shared in Muhammad's private decisions and it is an open fact that Muhammad was influenced by their advice.

Malcolm suspected that John Ali was the Iago of the drama. If true—and more than once Malcolm told me it was true—the intrigue is a classic one. Little has been written about the relationship between John Ali and Malcolm but some information is available:

Ali is from Philadelphia and it is believed that he and Malcolm joined forces when Malcolm arrived in Philadelphia to establish a Mosque. In stark contrast to Malcolm, John Ali is a quiet, efficient master of organizational details. He seldom, if ever, smiles. I met Ali while preparing "The Hate That Hate Produced." He was Malcolm's top advisor and secretary of the New York Mosque as well. The two men were inseparable, both in body and mind. Malcolm and his wife shared a home in Queens with Ali and his family. The home was the scene of the first police encounter with the Black Muslims in New York. After a heated trial, a Queens jury ruled that the police had entered the home illegally and terrorized pregnant women and children.

Subsequently John Ali quit New York and became secretary of the entire Black Muslim organization. His office was in Chicago with Elijah Muhammad. There have been scores of speculations as to why this move was made. My own view is that it was a simple matter of an organization deploying its best talent to an important national post. The important point is that the relationship beween the two men began to fragment; things began to happen to Malcolm. The newspaper was taken from Malcolm and moved to Chicago under Ali; Malcolm's activities and speeches received progressively less and less coverage in the paper. Elijah Muhammad was seriously ill and the ugly issue of succession that always plagues such an organization set off rumors of a conspiracy between Ali and certain members of Elijah's family.

Malcolm and I discussed the matter on several occasions and he flatly denied any ambition to succeed Elijah. Now that Malcolm has written his autobiography it is clear that his denials were honest and that the organization was being plagued by a deep doctrinal rift. Malcolm was in alliance with Akbar Muhammad and it now appears that he wished to see Akbar succeed his father. After all

Akbar had studied true Islam in Cairo and together he and Malcolm could have given the organization a sounder doctrine. Others around Muhammad were pressing for a more "conventional" successor, perhaps Elijah's youngest son, Wallace.

Muhammad's health improved and the question of succession was muted. However the infighting left serious scars on both Malcolm and the inner circle of the organization. The entire matter surfaced in early 1963.

The Amsterdam News, a Harlem weekly, carried an article by James Booker to the effect that "minor" differences had developed between Malcolm and Elijah Muhammad. During a tape recorded interview with me Malcolm mentioned the article and then exploded with fury:

MALCOLM: "It's a lie. Any article that says there is a 'minor' difference between Mr. Muhammad and me is a lie. There is no such thing as a 'minor' difference with the Messenger. Any difference with him is major. It is a lie, a lie, a lie. Somebody paid (the author) to write. I was up there in his office yesterday and I was ready to waste (harm, or kill) him for that. He planted a false seed, and it could start trouble. He (the author) knows my telephone number. If he ran on talk of a difference between men and the Messenger, he could have called me. No, he went ahead and printed this lie.

"He was not there, but I told the editor of the paper that I was out to find him; I told them to call the police then, because as soon as I found the man who wrote this I was going to do him in.

"How could there be any difference between the Messenger and me? I am his slave, his servant, his son. He is the leader, the only spokesman for the Black Muslims.

"But I will tell you this: The Messenger has seen God. He was with Allah and was given divine patience with the devil. He is willing to wait for Allah to deal with this devil. Well, sir, the rest of us Black Muslims have not seen God. We don't have this gift of divine patience with the devil. The younger Black Muslims want to see some action."

As Malcolm himself admitted, he was not being honest. There were differences, and they were major. The unmistakable thrust of the latter portion of Malcolm's rejoinder is that younger Black Muslims were impatient with the leadership of Elijah, the man who had seen God and was thus lenient with the white devil. Under new leadership, the statement suggests, the anxious young turks would "see some action."

Three weeks after the interview Malcolm called me.

"I have something to tell you," he said. "Meet me you know where."

I hastened to our private meeting place in an obscure Queens restaurant.

"The rumors are true," Malcolm told me. "Somebody in the Chicago office is out to get me."

"Who is it?" I asked.

"It's John!"

The word "John" was uttered in a forced and pained whisper.

Malcolm was a shaken man that day. He was in deep trouble with the Black Muslim organization and he knew it. More, he was convinced that the knife in his back had been plunged and twisted by his close friend and brother.

Meanwhile, Martin Luther King's organization's essential validity was never in question even though many doubted that a church-related com-

bine could carry out a broad civil rights movement.
And Martin had been more than validated; he was
Time magazine's Man of The Year and the winner
of the Nobel Peace Prize. The overwhelming majority of Negroes named him their most effective
leader.

Although Martin and Malcolm agreed that ghetto
rioting was imminent they sharply disagreed on the
question of what to do about it. Martin saw the
solution as "integration," the full dispersing of the
black population into the general American social
and economic mainstream; Malcolm—in the name
of Elijah Muhammad—called for complete "separation" of the races. On this particular point Malcolm
was more of a segregationist than white Southerners; he called for a separate state which would
be inhabited by and belong to the American Negro.

It is not known when Elijah Muhammad first
came upon the notion of a separate state and
commanded all of his ministers to join in the call
for such a venture. My first encounter with the
notion came as Malcolm and I were working on the
third issue of the Black Muslim newspaper, then
known as the *Islamic News*. After having edited
copy detailing the exploits of Yacob, the mad black
scientist whom Elijah Muhammad accuses of having created white people, I was prepared for almost
anything. Yet when Malcolm called me and said he
wanted a headline "We Must Have Land Of Our
Own" I wondered if both he and I had not lost our
senses. Malcolm rushed to join me at the printing
plant and the entire front page was rewritten. The
thrust of the call for a separate state was this: The
American government should set aside one, or
more, states for the black man. All of the white
people now living in these states would be moved

out and all Negroes, regardless of where they are now living, would be moved in. All black Americans would then become Muslims and, of course, Elijah would be the Allah-appointed governor. The final assumption was that the American government would not only give black men "some states but that Washington would give black men enough seed money to go for themselves."

My first reaction was to view the matter as a joke; little did I realize that the separate states doctrine came directly from Muhammad and was to become one of the central tenets of the Black Muslim orthodoxy. Shortly after the paper appeared Malcolm raised the question of separate states in a debate against me at Yale University. He demanded a state; I offered him Mississippi; he refused to take it.

Seriously viewed, the separate states doctrine was undergirded by the concept that before people could achieve full freedom they must have a homeland, an Israel. This notion obsessed Malcolm and he continued to preach it even after he quit the Black Muslim movement. This is how Malcolm stated the case for separate black states before an audience at Yale University:

"The cry of the black man in Africa for the return of his own land is so widespread, so unrelenting, so uncompromising ... it stands to reason that only God Himself is inspiring him and driving him onward in this spirit of freedom. If God has made the black man in Africa realize he cannot rest until he has some land of his own ... surely that same God will look westward toward America and see 20 million black people here, SECOND-CLASS CITIZENS, who are also in dire need of some land that we can call our own.

"If Mr. Muhammad says 'some land of our own' is God's solution to this grave race problem, why land? Why is land so important to everyone today?

"The white man in Great Britain could once boast that his control extended over so much of the black man's land that the sun never set on the British Empire. Today, when the sun rises, we can hardly find the British Empire.

"How important is land? Well, look what happened to the British Empire when she lost the lands she had colonized in Asia: lands like India, China, Burma, Malaya, etc. . . . her inability to continue robbing Asia of the natural resources produced by the land almost wrecked the British economy, decreased her military strength and her political prestige so low she could no longer use 'force' to hold her African colonies.

"As her grip on the black man's land loosened, Britain dwindled. Loss of land meant loss of Empire . . . loss of wealth, power, and of prestige."

Malcolm's argument was as brilliant as it was wrong. Had he been a leader of black Africans seeking the end of colonialism his urging would have made complete sense. But as a spokesman for black men in an ethnically jumbled America Malcolm made a court jester of himself by becoming the chief propagandist for Elijah's separate states scheme. Indeed, it was this issue that caused many Negroes to charge that the Black Muslim movement was being financed by white segregationists—specifically oil magnate H. L. Hunt of Dallas, Texas.

The Malcolm X of that era was the bitter polemicist who never eschewed an opportunity to publicly attack established Negro leaders. Having stated his case for separate states before the Yale audience

Malcolm went on to deliver a scathing and extended attack on Negro leadership; his unmistakable target was Martin Luther King:

"The New York Tribune, in an editorial (February 5, 1960), pointed out that out of 11 million qualified Negro voters, only 2,700,000 actually took time to vote. This means that, roughly speaking, only 3 million of the 11 million Negroes who are qualified to vote take an active part ... and the remaining 8 million remain voluntarily inactive, and yet it is this small minority of Negro voters who help determine who will be the next president.

"If who will be the next president can be influenced by 3 million Negro voters, it is easy to see why the presidential candidates of both political parties put on such a false show with the civil rights bill, and with promises of integration. They must woo or impress the 3 million voting Negroes who are the actual 'integration seekers.'

"If so much fuss is made over these 3 million 'integration seekers,' what would the presidential candidates have to do to appease the 8 million non-voting if they ever decided to become politically active in the election year?

"Who are the 8 million non-voting Negroes, what do they want, and why don't they vote?

"The 3 million voters are the so-called middle-(or high-)class Negroes, referred to by Howard University Sociology Professor E. Franklin Frazier as the *Black Bourgeoisie,* who have been educated to think as patriotic individualists, with no racial pride '... who believe in, and look forward to, the future integrated-intermarried' society promised them by the Negro politicians ... and therefore, this 'integration-minded' 3 million remain an active part of the white-controlled political parties. But it must never be overlooked, that these 3 million integration seekers are only a small minority of the 11 million qualified voters.

"The 8 million non-voting Negroes are the majority, the downtrodden black masses. They have refused to vote, or to take part in politics, because they reject the Uncle Tom approach of the 'clergy-politician' leadership that has been hand-picked for the American Negroes by the white man himself.

"The clergy-politician leadership does not speak for the Negro majority; they don't speak for the black masses. They speak for the *Black Bourgeoisie*, the 'brainwashed' (white-minded) middle-class minority . . . who, because they are ashamed of black, and don't want to be identified with black or as being black, are seeking to lose this 'identity' by mingling, mixing, intermarrying, and integrating with the white man.

"The race problem cannot be solved by listening to this white-minded (brainwashed) minority. The white man must try to learn what does the majority want. The next president would be wise to try and learn what the black masses want. And, the only way to find this out is by listening to the man who speaks for the black masses of America.

"I declare to you and to the entire world, that the man here in America who speaks for the majority, the downtrodden, dissatisfied black masses . . . is this same man whom so many thousands of our people are flocking toward to see and hear . . . this same Mr. Muhammad who is labeled by you as a Black Supremacist, and as a Racist!

"If the 3 million middle-class Negroes are casting their ballots for integration and intermarriage . . . what do the non-voting black masses who are in the minority want? Find out what the black masses want, and then perhaps American's grave race problem can be solved.

"The black masses are tired of following these hand-picked Negro 'leaders' who sound like professional beggars, as they cry year after year for white America to accept us as first-class citizens.

"Since this clergy-politician 'Leadership,' which was carefully hand-picked for us by the white man, has failed to solve the problem for the downtrodden black masses . . . God Himself has stepped into the picture, and has made Messenger Elijah Muhammad a wise, fearless, and uncompromising spokesman for the 20 million black people here in America, who, behind the Divine Leadership of this man of God, will now never be satisfied until we have a home in a land that we can proudly call our own."

The tragedy of the dialogue between Malcolm and Martin was that like a two-edged sword, it cut both ways. All too many people, black and white, had come to view "integration" as an attempt by middle-class blacks to become white men. This, of course, was not true. And Malcolm's call for a separate black state (or states) was both impractical and foolish.

The issue at bay was the Negro's realistic role in American life. And it was abundantly evident—even then—that the Negro would not completely "integrate" according to Martin Luther King's dream nor would he "separate" and achieve Malcolm's urging.

TEN

"DE LAWD" AND THE ORGANIZATION

His close inner circle called him "De Lawd," and wherever Martin Luther King, Jr. was, the *movement* was in the midst of him; for Martin King was the movement.

Along the streets of Montgomery in 1955, one could hear people ask, "Where is the *movement* tonight?"

"At Dexter Avenue," the reply would be. That meant that the nightly meeting in support of the bus boycott would be held at the Dexter Avenue Church. That *movement* rendered bus segregation a thing of the past.

"Honey," a Negro woman in Birmingham said to a neighbor, "the movement is out in the streets with the dogs and fire hoses." And that is precisely where we were, out in the streets generating creative tension with Bull Connor. That *movement* was the death knell of lunch-counter segregation.

"The white folks have put the whole *movement* in jail!" a Selma woman exclaimed. Indeed a good deal of the *movement*, including Martin King and Ralph Abernathy, was in jail. But in the wake of their suffering and marching the nation got a new and sweeping civil rights bill.

The Southern Christian Leadership Conference was—and is—an umbrella organization. It has a staff of about a dozen people who kept the shop while Martin both answered and generated "Macedonian calls." Martin's early successes inspired many Negro ministers and other professionals in various Southern cities to launch their own *movements* against segregation. Invariably, the local leaders would be scorned and brutalized by their police and then the "Macedonian call" would go out for Martin and his lieutenants to come in and give assistance. Sometimes the local leaders would seek Martin's presence. On other occasions Martin would arrange to be called in. In either case the pattern was almost unchanging: Usually the local leader would have been jailed and released on bond by the time Martin came on the scene. With the local leader at his side Martin would then deliver a series of revivalistic civil rights sermons.

"I got on my marching shoes!" Martin would shout.

"Yes, Lord, me too," the people answered back.

"I woke up this morning with my mind stayed on freedom!"

"Preach, doctor, preach."

"I ain't going to let nobody turn me round!"

"Let's march, brother; we are with you!"

"If the road to freedom leads through the jail house—if the road to freedom leads through the jail house, then turnkey swing wide the gates!"

"Amen; praise the Lord!"

"Some of you are afraid," Martin told them.

"That's right; that's right."

"Some of you are contented."

"Speak, speak, speak," the masses shouted as they eyed the embarrassed black teachers and doctors in the audience.

"But if you won't go," Martin shouted.

"Don't hinder me!" the people joined in as they shared the climax.

At this juncture the organ or the piano struck the first soft notes of "We Shall Overcome."

"We will march nonviolently," Martin continued. "We shall force this nation, this city, this world, to face its own conscience."

"Yes, Lord!"

"We will make the God of love in the white man triumphant over the Satan of segregation that is in him."

"Yes, yes."

"The struggle is not between black and white!"

"No, no," the people confirmed.

"But between good and evil."

"That's it; that's it."

"And whenever good and evil have a confrontation, good will win!"

"Yes, Lord."

"For God is not dead; I know because I can feel him . . ."

"Deep in my soul!" the people shout completing the line from the Negro spiritual.

Then, arm in arm with the local leader, Martin led the people into the streets to face dogs, tear gas, fire hoses and, frequently, brutality and additional jailing. With a few rare exceptions, the nonviolent ploy worked. The issue was settled either on local terms or through federal action. In his last years Martin's goal was federal legislation that would pre-empt the local issue and set a pattern for the nation as a whole.

This was the *movement* at its best, the leading of thousands of people into the streets to face danger for the sake of a freedom promised and written large in America's founding documents. Ofttimes local white judges would give King an additional weapon: they would enjoin him from marching and thus create a second issue—the right of the people to protest peacefully. This is precisely the path Memphis was traveling when King was assassinated. The garbage collectors, ninety-five percent of whom are black, struck against the city for higher wages; weeks of protest passed with no progress, and scorn and recriminations from the white power structure. Then Martin answered a call to come in and give aid; his first march was flecked by violence for reasons I will discuss later. Martin was determined to carry out a peaceful march and received the added impetus he needed when a local judge enjoined him from marching.

"I do not believe the injunction is constitutional." Martin told a cheering crowd. "And I will not obey an illegal court order."

The pattern was the classic one and it was clear that Martin was preparing the people, and himself, for jail. The creative tension was building; it was just a matter of time before officials, either in Memphis or in Washington, would have to resolve the issue and restore calm.

As seen on television, the *movement* was an exciting and probing maneuver. The behind the scenes control of the demonstrations was yet a different matter.

Local leaders had created the issue long before Martin arrived in town. Inevitably, Martin became the focal point of national attention, ofttimes creating envy and jealousy. Black leadership is heady business and there is something about the prospect of appearing on "Meet The Press," and then making the "Liberal" circuit as a banquet speaker, that causes some men to do unusual things. Then there was the organizational question. Martin's staff was better educated and more experienced than the lieutenants of the local organizations they moved in to assist. Invariably, as the United States did to the government in Saigon, Martin's people would move in and assume the full direction of the *movement*. Many local leaders resented this; some of them withdrew and refused to participate further.

Money always breeds trouble. Once Martin King moved into a city and began demonstrations, thousands of people from around the world would send money, ofttimes loose cash, to finance the effort. To whom—what organization, that is—did this money really belong? The local movements were always penniless and the leaders felt the money should go into their coffers; Martin's earlier lieutenants felt they should manage the funds and pay only those local expenses they had authorized. In his last years, Martin's staff developed a method of avoiding this conflict; criticism based on the handling of money died out.

The Albany Movement of 1961, one of Martin King's true failures, provides an excellent insight into the strains and conflicts that inevitably accrued to the kind of organization Martin structured. The NAACP Youth Council of Albany elected to integrate bus terminal facilities in that Georgia city. They had a ready-made cause and plenty of marching bodies. A Negro state college was located there and the black servicemen stationed at the army base in Albany had been complaining about local segregated services for fifteen years. Following the NAACP tactic, the students made a quiet test; they sought service at the bus station and were refused. Once the issue was joined, the youths took the matter to court and settled back to what would have been a two or three year wait for a Supreme Court decision.

The Albany situation came to the attention of the Student Nonviolent Coordinating Committee in Atlanta, a student-oriented civil rights group that had been midwifed and financed by King's organization. SNCC launched "freedom rides" into Albany and mobilized local Negroes in support of the freedom riders. This put SNCC—and, tangently, Martin King—in direct odds with the NAACP. Hundreds of students, black and white, were jailed for violating state and local segregation laws. As the jailings and beatings mounted in Albany, blacks of all classes began to demonstrate in the streets; they were solidly behind the students. To avoid further conflict the Albany Movement was created; this allowed all of the groups to work together and received equal acclaim. Dr. G. T. Anderson, a local physician and black leader, was named head of the movement. Another Montgomery was in the making and the nation's eyes began to focus on Albany.

At this jucture Martin King and Wyatt Walker, then his principal aide, flew in to Albany to give "aid and assistance." Martin's presence as an inspirational leader coupled with his willingness to endure jail was most welcome. But Walker had the power, the green power; SNCC was simply the conduit through which King's organization had financed the Albany Movement. The conflict was overshadowed, however, when world opinion condemned the jailing of Martin and Dr. Anderson. Tension mounted as both King and Anderson announced that they would stay in jail "until a change came." The secondary leadership carried out daily negotiations with the town fathers and always came away empty-handed. The city verged on a race riot and some definitive action would have occurred had Martin remained in jail as he promised. To everyone's dismay King elected to accept bond and walk out of jail. The chain that kept the creative tension was thus snapped and the bus station facilities were not integrated.

This was King's most difficult hour; he was loudly criticized in every black community and people vowed never to follow him again. I dealt with this incident in my book *The Negro Revolt* and commented that Martin elected to quit jail in order to avoid a more difficult and embarrassing development. Martin jokingly promised he would not be nonviolent with me if I printed the story. Thousands of readers have written me asking for the details. Now that Martin is eternally asleep I can reveal some of the details, not all of them for they involve people yet alive and—in a sense—innocent.

There were several key black leaders in Albany. The evidence suggests that one of them became mentally ill as a result of the days of danger and stress. During the march that led to King's jailing, this particular leader began to view himself as a holy man, perhaps Jesus; as he marched along with King he began making gestures which indicated that in his own mind he was sprinkling holy water on the black crowds that lined the sidewalk and cheered. Once in jail this leader's illusions of holy grandeur expanded to the point that, again in his own mind, he began to walk on water and feed a multitude of five thousand with the slice of bread the jailer brought him for supper. Martin and others of those jailed conferred and agreed that it would be disastrous for the movement if the white jailer discovered and informed the world that one of the key local black leaders was mentally ill. During jail visits, Martin's associates all agreed and every effort was made to persuade the man to accept bond. The local leader was adamant; he refused to quit jail as long as Martin remained in confinement. Martin had invited religious leaders from all over America to come to Albany and spend Christmas in jail with him. Scores were preparing to do just that.

Then one night the jailer noticed the black leader's peculiar behavior.

"That nigger acts like he done gone crazy!" the jailer observed within Martin's hearing. The following day Martin came out on bond and brought the ill leader with him. The leader in question soon left Albany and, after several months in a rest home, is completely recovered.

"A Major Defeat For Martin Luther King" the *New York Tribune* headline said of Albany. Perhaps it was, but Martin went on to march again in Birmingham. And in Birmingham the pattern of organizational conflict continued as King upstaged the Reverend Fred Shuttlesworth, the local black leader. But the two men had been friends for years and the problems never became personal or abrasive. More significantly, the Birmingham demonstrations were a major factor in bringing about federal legislation outlawing segregation in interstate commerce. Finally, then, the bus station facilities in Albany were integrated.

Like most inspirational and creative men, Martin King was not an effective administrator. He was apt to announce programs on the spur of the moment and without careful planning, whenever "the spirit moved" him. In his early days he had several such men as his top aides, and the combination led to serious organizational problems. The Southern Christian Leadership Conference's annual convention of 1961 in Nashville is a case in point. During a press conference there, King had his aide, at that time the Reverend James Lawson, at his side.

"What is the program of your organization for the next year?" a reporter asked.

King deferred to Lawson who was program director of SCLC and Lawson replied, "We plan to send a nonviolent army through the South next year!"

The white reporter swallowed hard and then asked, "How many will be in your army?"

"Oh," Lawson answered, "I would say about a quarter of a million Negroes."

This was the first—and last—anybody but Lawson, including Martin Luther King, had ever heard about the nonviolent army of a quarter of a million blacks that would march through the South.

Perhaps the spirit of the times was such that these two traits, poor planning and the tendency to enter movements others already have underway, would one day produce Martin's gravest difficulties. After James Meredith was shot during his 1966 March through Mississippi, Martin and other black leaders decided to take up the march at the spot where the not too seriously wounded Meredith fell. Along with Martin on the march was Stokely Carmichael . . . the details of that march are a part of a future chapter but the climax is part of the organizational difficulties we are now considering. King, the head of SCLC, Carmichael, the leader of SNCC, and Floyd McKissick, the director of CORE, formed a coalition to complete Meredith's march. The creative tension they induced along the highway was second only to the tension that was developing among the triumvirate itself. McKissick and Carmichael objected to the presence of white sympathizers who wanted to join the march; Martin of course, insisted upon an integrated march. But this was not the gut issue; as they marched deeper into Mississippi the three men became absorbed in a debilitating argument over the basic philosophy that would undermine the civil rights movement from that point forward. The group marched into Greenwood, Mississippi, where hundreds had gathered in a local park for a rally. And it was there that Carmichael mounted the platform and issued his now famous and rasping call for "Black Power!"

Later Carmichael was to confess that he raised the issue during the march to get national attention; then he added, "Martin, I deliberately raised the issue here to force you to take a stand for black power."

Martin smiled dryly and then commented, "I have been used before; one more time will not hurt."

Perhaps it did not hurt, but Martin Luther King was to spend the remainder of his life and all of his energies attempting to combat the forces unleashed by Carmichael's strident call for "Black Power." To counteract these rioting forces, Martin determined to lead a "poor people's" march on Washington during the spring and early summer of 1968. Such skilled civil rights organizers as Bayard Rustin, the person who manned the March On Washington, strongly advised King against the effort; their argument was that black people are now too volatile for such a march to be staged and that, as presented to a Miami planning conference, the march was poorly organized. Martin insisted and Rustin lapsed into silent opposition.

At this writing, one week after Martin's death, it is too early to fully evaluate Memphis. But it seems clear that he viewed Memphis as an opportunity to aid the garbage workers as well as a training ground for the march he was to carry out in Washington. As Martin himself admitted, the first Memphis march was not properly organized. He promised both God and the people he would do better the next time around.

It was his ability to inspire people, not his organizational genius, that caused millions to give Martin Luther King, Jr. their total love and loyalty. In the beginning many suspected him of pursuing personal grandeur; but after he had climbed every mountain and then went on to die fighting for garbage men, history can only assess him as a man of total conviction.

His close associates knew this about him from the onset. This is why they called him "De Lawd."

ELEVEN

THE CHICKENS CAME HOME TO ROOST

"The time is out of joint," Hamlet mused, "O cursed spite, that ever I was born to set it right!"

So it was with both Malcolm X and Martin Luther King, Jr. They both had so much to offer, so much to live for, so many reasons to die quietly in bed when they were old and grey. Yet, and this is true of all too many brilliant black men, American society murdered them by insisting that they consume and preoccupy their own lives with the struggle against racism. The time is indeed out of joint; both Malcolm and Martin were obsessed with the conviction that they had been sent to set it right.

Nineteen-sixty-four was the first year of the long, hot summers. For Malcolm it was the last of his summers on earth. For Martin it was a time of planning for the Selma (Alabama) Movement, the last of Martin's truly heroic demonstrations. For both men it was a time of organizational troubling and private reevaluation.

Malcolm X's troubles had become public discussion late in 1963. Following the assassination of John F. Kennedy on November 22nd of that same year Elijah Muhammad issued strict orders—two fiats, in fact—to all his ministers that they make no comment whatsoever on the assassination. The blanket directive, of course, included Malcolm X. But long before the assassination of Kennedy, Elijah Muhammad had scheduled a major rally in

New York: the New York Temple had paid a handsome fee to rent Manhattan Center for the occasion. As he had done several times since his 1961 illness, Muhammad elected not to address the New York rally. Malcolm and his fellow members of Temple Number Seven were unable to recoup the rental fee for the hall and Elijah authorized Malcolm to speak rather than allow the event to become a total financial loss. The blunt fact is that both Muslims and non-Muslims had become accustomed to the fact that Elijah seldom kept publicized appearances and that Malcolm—whom everybody wanted to hear in the first place—substituted.

There was nothing unusual about the Manhattan Garden event, then, except for the fact that it occurred after the assassination of President Kennedy. Malcolm was at his fulminating best; taking as a text "as you sow, so shall you reap," he went on to give the American white man hell, to predict that in hell is precisely where the white man will end up. Then came the question and answer period, a Malcolm innovation that Elijah never would have carried out in public.

If the record of what occurred next is to be corrected we must take note of the fact that Malcolm was aware of the following: He knew he was in trouble with the Black Muslim organization and he was convinced that John Ali was his tormentor; Malcolm also knew that he was under strict orders from Muhammad NOT to comment on the assassination.

The give-and-take period had hardly begun when someone asked Malcolm to comment on the assassination. The exact transcript of Malcolm's reply has never been published. What was reported was that Malcolm said "the chickens have come home to roost." The public press was still remembering Malcolm's remarks in which he had God slapping down a plane loaded with white Southerners as retribution for the killing of Black Muslims in Los Angeles, and reporters interpreted Malcolm's comment as a statement of jubilance over Kennedy's death. The press was justified in its handling of Malcolm's remarks. He literally invited misinterpretation by saying, "Being an old farm boy myself, chickens coming home to roost never did make me sad; they've always made me glad."

The week after Malcolm had been suspended by Elijah Muhammad, I interviewed him over coffee at Temple Number Seven Restaurant along Lenox Avenue. The transcript of the interview shows that the question of the suspension and the "chickens have come home to roost" speech arose after Malcolm had once again unleashed a bitter attack on the American white man's violence-laden history.

MALCOLM X: I have spoken on this many times, and I am sure you know what The Honorable Elijah Muhammad teaches on this. But since we are on record I will—as they sometimes say in Harlem —make it plain.

Now, sir, God is going to punish this wicked devil for his misdeeds toward black people. Just as plagues were visited on Pharaoh so will pestilences and disaster be visited on the white man. Why, it has already started: God has begun to send them heat when they expect cold; he sends them cold when they expect heat. Their crops are dying, their children are being born with all kinds of deformities, the rivers and the lakes are coming out of the belly of the earth to wash them away.

Not only that, but God has started slapping their planes down from the sky. Last year (1962) God

brought down one of their planes loaded with
crackers whose fathers had lynched your and my
brothers and sisters. They were from your state,
Lomax, down there in Georgia where both you and
Mr. Muhammad come from. Now, long before that
plane crash, I predicted (in Los Angeles) that God
was going to strike back at the devil for the way
white cops brutalized our brothers in Los Angeles.
When the plane fell, I said this was God's way of
letting his wrath be known. I said much the same
thing when that submarine—the Thresher—went
down to the bottom of the sea. Now for this I was
called names—some of these Uncle Tom Negroes
rushed into print to condemn me for what I had
said. But what was wrong with what I said? Everybody has a God and believes that His God will
deliver him and protect him from his enemies! Why
can't the black man have a God? What's so wrong
when a black man says his God will protect him
from his white foe? If Jehovah can slay Philistines
for the Jews, why can't Allah slay crackers for the
so-called Negro?

LOMAX: Is that the reasoning behind your remark
after the assassination of President Kennedy? You
are reported to have said that Kennedy's death was
an instance of "chickens coming home to roost."

MALCOLM X: Yes, but let's clear up what I said. I
did not say that Kennedy's death was a reason for
rejoicing. That is not what I meant at all. Rather, I
meant that the death of Kennedy was the result of a
long line of violent acts, the culmination of hate
and suspicion and doubt in this country. You see,
Lomax, this country has allowed white people to
kill and brutalize those they don't like. The assassination of Kennedy is a result of that way of life
and thinking. The chickens came home to roost;

that's all there is to it. America—at the death of the president—just reaped what it had been sowing.

LOMAX: But you were disciplined for making these remarks; The Honorable Elijah Muhammad has publicly rebuked you and has ordered you not to speak in public until further notice.

MALCOLM X: This is true. I was wrong; The Messenger had warned me not to say anything about the death of the president, and I omitted any reference to that tragedy in my main speech. But during a question-and-answer period someone asked about the meaning of the Kennedy assassination, and I said it was a case of chickens coming home to roost. Now about that suspension—it's just as if you have cut off a radio. The radio is still there, but it makes no sound. You can cut it back on when it pleases you.

LOMAX: How long do you think this suspension will last?

MALCOLM X: Only The Honorable Elijah Muhammad can answer that. I don't think it will be permanent.

LOMAX: Then you do expect to return to your duties?

MALCOLM: Yes, sir.

LOMAX: And you will continue to preach separation from the white man?

MALCOLM X: Yes, sir.

Wordiness was part of Malcolm's undoing. Rap Brown said it better and with no risk of being misunderstood: "Violence is as American as apple pie."

The question to ponder, then, is why Malcolm said anything at all. He knew his enemies were after him; he knew Elijah had forbade him to comment on the assassination. Why would he run such a risk?

Other than Vice President Hubert Humphrey, Malcolm X was the most compulsive public talker I have ever encountered. He could not resist the temptation to speak for the public record. When asked a question he compulsively responded. He ofttimes did not tell the truth but he never could say "no comment."

Malcolm's comment was little more than the doctrine Elijah Muhammad himself preaches. It will be recalled that during his televised interview with me Muhammad said all white men without exceptions were devils and that they would come to a bloody doom by 1970. But Malcolm was clearly guilty of flouting Muhammad's command that none of his ministers address themselves to the question of the assassination of John F. Kennedy.

It is clear that Malcolm's enemies seized upon this blunder to bring the mighty "Big Red" down. It is an insight into Muhammad, into his relationship to Malcolm, that only after Malcolm executed a public act of defiance did Elijah yield to the Black Muslim inner-circle members who willed the end of Minister Malcolm X.

I sat drinking coffee with Malcolm at the Temple Number Seven Restaurant in Harlem long after his ninety-day suspension had been imposed. Malcolm had been silenced, forbidden to talk to reporters. Yet we sat there in the restaurant talking as John X and several other members of the "Fruit" I had come to know looked on.

"How long will the suspension last?" I asked Malcolm.

"It better not last too long," Malcolm said. "I'm thinking about making a move on my own."

Even then Malcolm knew he would never be readmitted to the fold. Only several months later did he tell me that at the time we were talking in the restaurant he knew one of the "Fruit" looking on had been assigned to assassinate him.

Malcolm was plotting his next move. I was not the only one who knew it. Suffering out the days of his suspension Malcolm wrote a simple note to Alex Haley, his biographer: "You have not converted a man by silencing him. Viscount Morley." On the same night Malcolm sent Haley another note: "I was going downhill until he picked me up. Come to think of it maybe we picked each other up." Both comments obviously concerned his relationship with Elijah Muhammad.

As all concerned in the dispute—most of all Malcolm—well knew, Malcolm was not to be reinstated. It came as a surprise to no one when Malcolm announced the formation of his own organization, the "Muslim Mosque, Inc." Malcolm seized the initiative and broke from Elijah Muhammad, the only father he ever really had. It was during this period that Malcolm exploded, "We had the best organization black men ever had. Niggers ruined it!" And—for Malcolm, that is—the "nigger" was John Ali.

No longer under Elijah's mystic canopy, Malcolm, like all religious fanatics, had to acquire a new unction unto himself; he had to go as near to God (Allah) as mortals can get and thus give himself authority before those who seek God by following a man who has been with God.

Malcolm X made the pilgrimage to Mecca on money he borrowed from his sister, Ella Collins.

From Mecca Malcolm wrote his much publicized letters in which he claimed to have discovered that not all white people are devils, that there are white Moslems. His autobiography contains a long and self-serving account of that period. My own duty is to discount these letters other than to say that at last Malcolm had found a way to publicly state, and philosophically justify, that which he had known from the onset of his career with the Black Muslims and Elijah Muhammad. What is valid is Malcolm's mystical account of the Mecca moment and his subsequent conferences with Arab and black African political leaders.

He is going through customs in Cairo and the key fails to open his suitcase. Out of fear that the officials may think he has a bomb inside he breaks open his suitcase. He suddenly realizes that the "white man" is a matter of religious conviction rather than of color; and King Faisal bluntly tells Malcolm that he has been preaching a false concept of Islam—as if Malcolm didn't know it.

But if Malcolm was on a religious retreat and being lectured to so was Martin Luther King. The planning for the Selma Movement was a stormy retreat during which the youthful members of the Student Nonviolent Coordinating Committee told him that nonviolent tactics were no longer effective. They went on to argue that the American white man simply would not respond to prayers, marches and nonviolent jailings. True, the black young people admitted, such marches result in far-sweeping civil rights laws, but white people have no intention of obeying such laws. More, the young militants added, the government is not going to prosecute white men for their lawlessness against black men.

Martin persisted in his march and Malcolm emerged from his Mecca ... The Selma march errupted into violence as white policemen used tear gas against black and white clergymen of all faiths, as well as nuns. Martin King was jailed, and key members of the Student Nonviolent Coordinating Committee invited Malcolm, who had come home and announced the formation of yet another organization that would take up the struggle of non-white men all over the earth, to address a Selma rally to protest Martin's imprisonment.

King's aides, particularly Andy Young, were deeply concerned that Malcolm might call for violence. Malcolm assured them he had no such intentions and then went on to say to Mrs. King, "I am here to help your husband. When I am finished the white man will be glad to release Dr. King from jail and deal with him."

That night Malcolm sat on the platform next to Mrs. King. He kept his word:

"I do not call for violence," Malcolm told the cheering crowd, "but if a man steps on my toes I will step on his. The white man had better be glad," Malcolm continued, "that Dr. King is leading a nonviolent revolution. There are those of us who are waiting for him to fail. Then the real revolution will begin."

Martin King was in jail; he did not hear Malcolm's speech. The two men did not meet that night. They never did meet. Yet it was the white man's refusal to obey the law that landed Martin King in jail; and it was the young black's impatience with the unlawful white man that caused them to bring Malcolm to Selma.

Martin Luther King and Malcolm X were moving closer together than even they knew.

The American white man's chickens were indeed coming home to roost.

TWELVE

MALCOLM X AND BLACK POWER

There is no more tragic a figure than that of the physician who correctly diagnosed a disease but is unable to persuade the people to accept his cure. So it was with Malcolm X. He correctly reasoned that white society, in the North as well as the South, would not "integrate" without a struggle, and that the struggle had to involve more than marches and hymn singing. Malcolm was the only black leader who had both the wisdom and the courage to predict that the summer of 1964 would be long, hot, and bloody. Correctly sensing the mood of the nation's black youth he pointed out that young Negroes in Jacksonville, Florida, were throwing Molotov cocktails and predicted this would be the wave of the future. Finally and most significantly, Malcolm realized that integration simply had no meaning to the black masses, and that they would soon seek power through new forms and methods.

We all knew that militant members of the Student Nonviolent Coordinating Committee were throwing soft stones at Martin Luther King, their organizational mentor; we knew that Malcolm's denunciation of nonviolence would not stop at the waters edge of "self-defense;" we knew that despite a spate of civil rights bills the economic plight of the black masses was growing worse, not better.

And Malcolm knew better than most of us that the youth of the ghetto were itching "for some action!"

During his years as a Black Muslim minister Malcolm had gotten loud cheers from black street corner youths when he made scathing attacks on the white man and hinted at violence. They applauded Brother Malcolm but they did not attend his Mosque; they did not become Black Muslims. Martin King was revered in the South, respected in the North, but—even then—the streets of Harlem were not the platform for an advocate of nonviolence.

There was a mood in the black ghetto then; it can only be described as "anti-institutionism," as a rejection of organized society and institutional trappings. The young blacks ceased to believe in the system. They wanted none of the police, of politicians, of settlement houses and social agencies; most of all they became completely anti-church. God and all of the followers were viewed as copouts.

Malcolm X read this mood correctly when he inveighed against organized Christianity calling it the instrument of oppression; Martin King understood the same mood when he tried unceasingly to awaken the consciences of white Christians by saying they must repent, reform, or die on the vine. Yet neither Martin nor Malcolm could extricate himself from his own religious trappings in a manner that would allow him to fashion a new movement around the new mood that was enveloping the black ghetto. Malcolm's transition period, the months during which he agonized his way out of the Black Muslim movement and into the founding of his own organization, provides a classic study of how a brilliant and potentially powerful leader failed to capture the confidence of his would-be followers:

Malcolm made his "chickens have come home to roost" speech on December 1, nine days after John F. Kennedy was assassinated. Elijah Muhammad imposed the ninety-day suspension on the next day, December 2. If Muhammad had really meant the suspension as a mere public reprimand, then Malcolm would be up and talking on March 3, 1964. But Malcolm began to doubt that Muhammad was candid about the suspension. First off Malcolm received word that Black Muslims who had been his closest associates had been assigned to assassinate him. He reasoned that only Elijah could issue such orders; why would Elijah have Malcolm murdered if he intended to reinstate him?

Elijah increased Malcolm's doubts by issuing statements saying that Malcolm would be reinstated if—and when—he "submits."

"But I already submitted," Malcolm told me. "I submitted at the very moment of the suspension. I told Mr. Muhammad, 'Sir, I submit one hundred percent.'"

On this point Malcolm cannot be doubted. Literally scores of news agencies called Malcolm the day after the suspension and their reports clearly show that he assumed the role of an errant child who gladly submits to the discipline of his father. Lapsing into the codes of his criminal past, Malcolm concluded that the confusion about his unwillingness to "submit" was a setup, that he was being cast as an outlaw and outcast whom loyal Black Muslims could murder with impunity.

Savior's Day, the major Black Muslim gathering of each year, was scheduled for Chicago on February 26, 1964. Malcolm telephoned Elijah Muhammad and asked just when, precisely, would his suspension end. Elijah replied that he would think the matter over and contact Malcolm by mail. When the written reply did arrive it left Malcolm's status under a darker cloud than ever. Even so, Malcolm waited and brooded. The convention was held without Malcolm; March 2, the end of the ninety-day period, came and passed; there was no word concerning reinstatement.

On March 8, 1964, Malcolm called a press conference and announced the formation of his own organization, The Muslim Mosque, Inc. "This will give us a religious base and the spiritual force necessary to rid our people of the vices that destroy the moral fiber of our community," Malcolm explained to the press.

Malcolm had swapped the myth for the legend. Assuming Malcolm had the kind of devoted and continuing following needed to form an organization—and he did not have that type of following—he never could have structured the organization on a religious basis. The troops that were available—the angry blacks of the ghetto, the disenchanted young civil rights workers in the South—simply were not to be commanded by a leader who talked in terms of God or Allah.

Malcolm realized that his base was flawed and limited and he went on to add social and economic planks to his organizational platform:

"I am prepared," Malcolm said, "to cooperate in local civil rights actions in the South and elsewhere and shall do so because every campaign for specific objectives can only heighten the political consciousness of the Negroes and intensify their identification against white society.

"There is no use deceiving ourselves," Malcolm

continued, "good education, housing and jobs are imperative for Negroes, and I shall support them in their fight to win these objectives. But I shall tell the Negroes that while these are necessary, they cannot solve the main Negro problem.

"I shall tell them what a revolution means—the French revolution, the American revolution, the Algerian revolution. There can be no revolution without bloodshed and it is nonsense to describe the civil rights movement as a revolution."

Malcolm issued his call but the black people did not answer; Malcolm founded his organization but there were few joiners. Why? I think the answer lies in the fact that Malcolm was still talking loud without doing anything. He failed to listen to his own dissertation on the nature of a true revolution; a people cannot carry out a revolution by rhetoric! Had Malcolm, instead, marshaled what forces he had at his command, selected a clear-cut goal and announced that if the evil was not corrected within, say, ten days, all hell would break loose in New York City—well, had Malcolm done that he would have changed the course of his own life and the pace of American history as well.

From Malcolm's own pen there emerges a clear example of what occurred. He describes a Harlem rally sponsored by several "middle-class" Negro leaders; Malcolm had said he would work with all groups dedicated to the aid of the black man and they invited him to speak. But as the rally progressed and speaker after speaker droned on, Malcolm became convinced that these leaders did not really want him there, that they had invited him only because they knew the announcement of his presence would draw a crowd. When his turn came Malcolm seized the microphone and denounced the

Negro leaders for exploiting him; then he announced that he was not going to speak. The black youth who had come to hear Malcolm began to yell insults at the black leaders; then they gathered in a crowd and it was clear trouble was imminent. Malcolm mounted the hood of a car and dispersed the angry black youths.

Many who observed that rally later felt that was Malcolm's last opportunity; that he flubbed it. The point being that by simply raising his voice and giving a command Malcolm could have led the youth and given them a rallying point, given them a sense of organization they could understand and launched an action-oriented program. Instead he ordered them to disperse and go home. It is difficult to believe that Malcolm really understood the psychology of these young blacks who clearly wanted "some action."

What precisely, was Malcolm up to? It was his indecisiveness and mercurially shifting philosophies during this period that caused many people—black and white—to openly say that Malcolm X had become a con man.

Had Malcolm X been a con man—and he most certainly had the background for it—he would not have died broke. I know he handled literally tens of thousands of Elijah Muhammad's dollars; yet he left Sister Betty, his wife, and his children homeless and penniless. Malcolm X was not a con man; he was a holy man, a kind of individual modern society finds even more difficult to understand. The ultimate evidence of Malcolm's true objectives lies in a period of weeks which, strangely enough, are bracketed by debates against me, one in Cleveland, Ohio, on April 3, 1964, the other in Chicago on May 23rd of the same year.

On April 3, 1964, Malcolm X journeyed to Cleveland to debate me. The debate was under the auspices of the Cleveland chapter of CORE and the issue to be resolved was "The Negro Revolt: Where Do We Go From Here?" For Malcolm and me it was a warm reunion; I had been stationed in Cleveland for several months where I was doing a television documentary for KYW on the Negro ghetto. (The thesis of my documentary was that Hough, the ghetto, was going to explode with a riot if something was not done immediately. The station officials concluded that I was a black madman and refused to air the telecast. Not only did the Hough area erupt in total violence the following summer but as I write these words—late July, 1968—Cleveland is seized by mini-war.)

Malcolm elected as his topic "The Ballot or The Bullet." That Malcolm would even suggest that black men employ the ballot amounted to an upheaval in his thinking. Black Muslims are rigidly forbidden to participate in politics, even from voting. But, even more significantly, a close study of Malcolm's speech reveals new insight into Malcolm's plans and objectives immediately after he severed his relationship with Elijah Muhammad.

Malcolm's attempts to form an independent organization had not resulted in the thousands of joiners he had expected. Not a single civil rights organization asked him to join its staff; none of them offered to work with Malcolm on a project he might have prescribed. Even more, Malcolm realized that he was too much of an evangelist to be burdened with the minute details of operating an organization, even if he could have established one.

Instead Malcolm carved out a unique course for himself. He projected himself as the "Billy Graham" of black nationalism. After giving one of the best definitions of black nationalism ever recorded, Malcolm went on to project himself as the evangelist of black nationalism who, like Paul, would go from city to city spreading the gospel under the egis of existing civil rights and black national organizations. Once Malcolm had saved souls he would turn them over to local leaders who would translate their new found black nationalist faith into black nationalist works.

After administering to me the humorous and brotherly spanking which was always my fare when we clashed in debate Malcolm began to take care of serious business:

"I would now like to say a few words about the Muslim Mosque, Inc. which we established a few weeks ago in New York. We keep our religion in the Mosque. After our religious services are over, then, as Muslims we become involved in political action, social action, and economic action. We become involved with anybody, anywhere, any time and in any manner that is designed to eliminate the evils, the political, economic and social evils that are afficting the people of our community.

". . . The political philosophy of black nationalism means that the black man should control the politics and the politicians of his own community.

". . . The economic philosophy of black nationalism (means) that we should control the economy of our community. Why should white people be running the stores of our community?

". . . The social philosophy of black nationalism only means that we have to get together and remove the evils, the vices, alcoholism, drug addiction and other evils that are destroying the moral fiber of our community."

Having thus defined black nationalist philosophy, Malcolm then went on to project his role as a black nationalist evangelist who could not only keep out of the hair of jealous civil rights leaders but, as a visiting man-of-the-truth, who could fill their local pews and coffers as well:

"I have watched how Billy Graham comes into a city, spreading what he calls the gospel of Christ, which is only white nationalism. That's what he is. Billy Graham is a white nationalist; I am a black nationalist. But just as it is the national tendency for leaders to be jealous and look upon a powerful figure like Graham with suspicion and envy, how is it possible for him to come into a city and get the cooperation of all the church leaders?

". . . Billy Graham comes in evangelizing the gospel of Christ, he evangelizes the gospel, he stirs everybody up, but he never tries to start a church, all the churches would be against him. So he just comes in talking about Christ and tells everybody who gets Christ to go to any church where Christ is; in this way the church cooperates with him. So we are going to take a page from his book.

". . . Our gospel is black nationalism. We are not going to threaten the existence of any organization. Anywhere there is a church preaching and practicing the gospel of black nationalism, join that church. If the NAACP is preaching and practicing black nationalism, join the NAACP. If CORE is spreading and preaching the gospel of black nationalism, join CORE. Join any organization that has a gospel that's for the uplift of the black man. And when you get into it and see them pussyfooting and compromising, pull out because that is not black nationalism. We'll find another one (organization to join)."

Following the debate a private party was held for Malcolm and me at the home of Attorney Zelma Alexander, one of the first Negro delegates to the United Nations. He and I both held court. As I recall it there were no white people there. Led on by Dr. Esque Brown the Black Bourgeoisie were the all of the social gathering. They set the stage for the fiery dialogue between Malcolm and me. This exchange was not recorded. I do remember that my thrust was that there should be no such thing as a "black community" and that if white society insisted upon it, then the relegated black should, as Malcolm proposed, insist upon controlling such a forced community. Malcolm's reply—and I am working from memory, not notes—was that white America would never accept total integration—my quest—and that white America would also continue to control black communities until such time as black men mounted the kind of violence necessary to drive them out.

Malcolm shared the dream I shared with Martin Luther King. But Malcolm understood—and was murdered too soon to know how right he was—that the dream for the middle-class Negroes would be a nightmare for the black masses.

Although the slogan "Black Power" was not in vogue during Malcolm's lifetime it is perfectly safe to say that were he alive today he would be in the forefront of its advocates. A careful reading of his last speeches shows them larded with substantive issues that comprise the black power doctrine; Malcolm felt that blacks should control their "own" community; he repeatedly called for Negro ownership of ghetto businesses; it was his total view that black politicians should be responsible only to their black constituents; although Malcolm became a

lukewarm integrationist (he even approved of interracial marriage) in his last days he still envisioned a
black community that would be under the political
and economic control of blacks. Most of all Malcolm hewed to the black power line in that he
welcomed whites to the struggle so long as they
formed themselves into a parallel organization to
work in the white community; they were not allowed to join either of the organizations Malcolm
founded.

The Malcolm who viewed himself as the Billy
Graham of the black nationalist movement was a
tragic figure. He was philosophically confused, physically spent and financially penniless. He was the
roving evangelist whom none invited to come and
conduct a revival. The central tragedy—from Malcolm's point of view, that is—was that Malcolm had
little, if any, rapport with the young black students
who were then laying the foundations of the black
power movement.

Malcolm's final failure was his inability to clarify
his thinking and formulate a new and creative
approach to the black man's problems. Instead Malcolm attempted to build his organizations and philosophy upon tired myths and ethnic assumptions as
ancient as they were unwarranted.

BLACK UNITY:

On the announcement of the founding of both of
his organizations Malcolm said, "We must have
black unity. We cannot think in terms of integration
until black men unite."

What, precisely, is "black unity?" The notion is a
myth that has plagued the American Negro since
slavery. Those who have preached this unrealistic
doctrine were obsessed with the idea that all black

Americans—regardless of religious, professional and economic differences—should come together as one, under one vine and fig tree as a single organization. So absurd is the notion involved that one is justified in employing absurd rhetoric to expose it. Assuming all black Americans did come together in one organization, where would they hold the convention? What conference hall can accommodate twenty million people?

More soberly, it was totally unrealistic of Malcolm to even suggest that entrenched and established blacks would abandon their various power bases for a new organization. The black unity issue arose late in the fifties, with the emergence of Martin Luther King as a national figure. Many wondered why the various civil rights organizations could not combine. After all the NAACP, CORE, The Urban League and King's SCLC shared the same goals; Why not unite? The reply was that each organization had its basic method of operation and should remain separate. Not even the offer of millions of dollars from white philanthropists could tempt the various civil rights leaders toward organizational unity. They certainly would not unite under Malcolm X.

By insisting upon this "black unity" doctrine Malcolm exposed himself to charges of being a "con man." People knew this was empty rhetoric and felt Malcolm was simply playing a dishonest game. Malcolm would have done well to study the young students who were then plotting and planning. These black militants never wasted their time and mental powers discussing black unity. Rather they realized that to bring about change one must assemble an organization of dedicated people, outline a program and execute it. It is but a historical fact that the few always bring about the liberation of the many.

SPIRITUAL BASE:

Malcolm X severed his relationship with Elijah Muhammad but he was unable to reorient his mind. To the very end Malcolm was exhorting blacks to eschew dope, pork, tobacco and riotious living. Central to his thinking was the conviction that only through inward cleanliness could a people achieve social and economic progress. So deeply ingrained was this notion that Malcolm justified the founding of a separate Muslim organization for blacks on the grounds that the situation of blacks was so grave that they could not work within the framework of orthodox Moslem mosques.

Much of this, as I have already suggested, was a hangover from Malcolm's Black Muslim days. But there is yet another factor involved, one few students of Malcolm have noticed: Malcolm was in the first stages of becoming a true revolutionary.

Contrary to popular belief revolutionaries are extremely conservative individuals and they tend to take on the puritanical ways of their opponents. Despite all of the talk about common sex in the Marxist doctrine there is little free sex in Russia. One of the first things Castro did when he came to power in Cuba was to close down the nightclubs, sweep the prostitutes off the streets, and clamp a lid on the fleshpots.

The revolution becomes the new theology. One sees it clearly in Israel. For twenty years the Israelis have been obsessed with a "nation building" theology; the people have little time to think of other matters. The point was succinctly made by a professor at Jerusalem's Hebrew University who said to me, "The function of education is to build the state of Israel."

Malcolm was groping for the same idea. What he was saying was that the American black man didn't have time for "sin" and "debauchery"; that every black man's every waking moment should be devoted to and consumed by the black revolution. Malcolm called this a "spiritual base" and he used Allah as his authority. But honestly viewed Malcolm was preaching a black theology constructed around trappings borrowed from orthodox Islam. Martin Luther King was preaching the same gospel and he built it around tenets borrowed from Christianity.

But in a practical sense the notion of a "spiritual base" was just as spurious a myth as the notion of "black unity." Had this been an instance of black Americans taking over a country under strong, authoritarian leadership, perhaps some type of revolutionary theology would have made sense. But in terms of the American Negro's experience the teaching made no sense at all.

SEPARATISM:

Again Malcolm allowed himself to become trapped in discounted myth. Malcolm's father died while laboring for Marcus Garvey's "Back to Africa" movement. The notion that the American Negro would return to Africa was a complete hoax and Garvey died in a con man's cell. As Elijah's evangelist Malcolm encountered people who literally laughed in his face when he suggested that the American government "give us some states where we can go for ourselves." The call for separate black states became a national joke.

In his statement of severance from Elijah Muhammad Malcolm said this:

"I still believe that Mr. Muhammad's analysis of the problem is the most realistic, and that his solution is the best one. This means that I too believe the best solution is complete separation, with our people going back home, to our own African homeland."

Following this remark Malcolm came under great pressure from close friends who urged to have done with myths. After some reflection Malcolm revised his position:

"A better word to use than separation is independence. This word separation is misused. The 13 colonies separated from England but they called it the Declaration of Independence; they don't call it the Declaration of Separation, they call it the Declaration of Independence. When you're independent of someone you can separate from them. If you can't separate from them it means you're not independent of them."

But words are hardly a substitute for a program. Malcolm was still lost in the murky myth-notion that somehow American blacks could either return to Africa or achieve an independent status here. He seems never to have understood how inseparably interlocked the races are in American society.

AFRO-AMERICAN UNITY:

This, of course, is the biggest myth of them all. Since slavery there have been those who preached the notion that the American Negro and the black Africans should unite. The assumption was that the Africans would through this union, rid the slaves of colonialism and that the Negro would accomplish full status in America—perhaps he would return to

Africa. The myth gained considerable acceptance as Africans brought down colonialism and marched into the halls of the United Nations. Hundreds of Negro women rushed to get African husbands and scores of Negro businessmen suddenly saw themselves becoming African millionaries.

Even then there were those of us who cautioned that there was little, if any, cultural unity between the American Negro and the black African. This was the thesis of my first book, *The Reluctant African*. Indeed, Malcolm X arranged for me to make the most valuable contacts he had in Africa.

And the myth did explode. Black Africa substituted economic colonialism for political colonialism; many black American women found themselves one of several wives in an African harem and suffered nervous breakdowns. But the greatest exercise in myth-shattering came when Negroes reaized that Africans were not willing to jeopardize their interests by becoming vocal about the American race problem.

Two things had been hoped for: We expected the Africans to take advantage of their United Nation's platform to denounce America for racism; secondly, we expected the African states to make the American race problem a matter of United Nations debate and action just as they were doing in the case of South Africa.

Neither hope came to fruition. Instead the African states lined up with the American State Department in return for generous loans. The African delegates were gracious to us in their homes but not one of them would take to the floor of the United Nations and demand an open investigation of the black man's plight in America. Malcolm and other black nationalists preached loud and long about "our African brothers," but not a single delegate would associate with the black nationalists; none came to the nationalists' street corner rallies.

One heretofore unpublicized incident illustrates what occurred. During his Black Muslim days Malcolm tried desperately to interest African delegates in the Muslim's program. The Nigerian ambassador to the United Nations agreed to attend a performance of the Black Muslim play, "The Trial," at Carnegie Hall. The ambassador, a devout Moslem, thought he was going to witness a religious drama based upon Islam. Instead he saw actors denouncing the white man as a "devil"; he heard a chorus singing "The White Man's Heaven is the Black Man's Hell." The ambassador got up and walked out.

Despite these experiences Malcolm could not rid himself of the myth of Afro-American unity. Knowing well that he could not get the ears of African ambassadors to the United Nations, Malcolm took his case to the summit meeting of the African heads of state in Cairo. It was a dejected Malcolm who sat in on the proceedings as an "observer" because his "African brothers" would not allow him to speak. More, Malcolm's fellow Moslem, Gamal Abdel Nasser, opened the conference by complimenting the American government for passing the civil rights act of 1964. The conferees finally decided to accept a memorandum from Malcolm. This document was a ringing plea for help and it provides a clear insight into the latter day Malcolm X:

Your Excellencies:
The Organization of Afro-American Unity has sent me to attend this historic African summit conference as an observer to represent the interests

of 22 million African-Americans whose human rights are being violated daily by the racism of American imperialists.

The Organization of Afro-American Unity (OAAU) has been formed by a cross-section of America's African-American community, and is patterned after the letter and spirit of the Organization of African Unity (OAU).

Just as the Organization of African Unity has called upon all African leaders to submerge their differences and unite on common objectives for the common good of all Africans—in America the Organization of Afro-American Unity has called upon Afro-American leaders to submerge their differences and find areas of agreement wherein we can work in unity for the good of the entire 22 million African-Americans.

Since the 22 million of us were originally Africans, who are now in America not by choice but only by a cruel accident in our history, we strongly believe that African problems are our problems, and our problems are African problems.

Your Excellencies:

We also believe that as heads of the Independent African States you are the shepherds of all African peoples everywhere, whether they are still at home on the mother continent or have been scattered abroad.

Some African leaders at this conference have implied that they have enough problems here on the mother continent without adding the Afro-American abroad.

With all due respect to your esteemed positions, I must remind all of you that the good shepherd will leave ninety-nine sheep, who are safe at home, to

go to the aid of the one who is lost and has fallen
into the clutches of the imperialist wolf.

We, in America, are your long-lost brothers and
sisters, and I am here only to remind you that our
problems are your problems. As the African-Americans "awaken" today, we find ourselves in a strange
land that has rejected us, and, like the prodigal son,
we are turning to our elder brothers for help. We
pray our pleas will not fall upon deaf ears.

We were taken forcibly in chains from this
mother continent and have now spent over 300
years in America, suffering the most inhuman forms
of physical and psychological tortures imaginable.

During the past ten years the entire world has
witnessed our men, women and children being
attacked and bitten by vicious police dogs, brutally
beaten by police clubs, and washed down the
sewers by high-pressure water hoses that would rip
the clothes from our bodies and the flesh from our
limbs.

And all of these inhuman atrocities have been
inflicted upon us by the American governmental
authorities, the police themselves, for no reason
other than we seek the recognition and respect
granted other human beings in America.

Your Excellencies:

The American government is either unable or
unwilling to protect the lives and property of your
22 million African-American brothers and sisters.
We stand defenseless, at the mercy of American
racists who murder us at will for no reason other
than we are black and of African descent.

Two black bodies were found in the Mississippi
River this week; last week an unarmed African-
American educator was murdered in cold blood in
Georgia; a few days before that three civil-rights

workers disappeared completely, perhaps murdered also, only because they were teaching our people in Mississippi how to vote and how to secure their political rights.

Our problems are your problems. We have lived for over 300 years in that American den of racist wolves in constant fear of losing life and limb. Recently, three students from Kenya were mistaken for American Negroes and were brutally beaten by New York police. Shortly after that, two diplomats from Uganda were also beaten by the New York City police, who mistook them for American Negroes.

If Africans are brutally beaten while only visiting in America, imagine the physical and psychological suffering received by your brothers and sisters who have lived there for over 300 years.

Our problem is your problem. No matter how much independence Africans get here on the mother continent, unless you wear your national dress at all times, when you visit America, you may be mistaken for one of us and suffer the same psychological humiliation and physical mutilation that is an everyday occurrence in our lives.

Your problems will never be fully solved until and unless ours are solved. You will never be fully respected until and unless we are also recognized and treated as human beings.

Our problem is your problem. It is not a Negro problem, nor an American problem. This is a world problem; a problem for humanity. It is not a problem of civil rights but a problem of human rights.

If the United States Supreme Court Justice Arthur Goldberg, a few weeks ago, could find legal grounds to threaten to bring Russia before the United Nations and charge her with violating the

*human rights of less than three million Russian
Jews, what makes our African brothers hesitate to
bring the United States government before the
United Nations and charge her with violating the
human rights of 22 million African-Americans?*

*We pray that our African brothers have not freed
themselves of European colonialism only to be
overcome and held in check now by American
dollarism. Don't let American racism be "legalized"
by American dollarism.*

*America is worse than South Africa, because not
only is America racist, but she also is deceitful and
hypocritical. South Africa preaches segregation and
practices segregation. She, at least, practices what
she preaches. America preaches integration and
practices segregation. She preaches one thing while
deceitfully practicing another.*

*South Africa is like a vicious wolf, openly hostile
towards black humanity. But America is cunning
like a fox, friendly and smiling, but even more
vicious and deadly than the wolf.*

*The wolf and the fox are both enemies of human-
ity; both are canine; both humiliate and mutilate
their victims. Both have the same objectives, but
differ only in methods.*

*If South Africa is guilty of violating the human
rights of Africans here on the mother continent,
then America is guilty of worse violations of the 22
million Africans on the American continent. And if
South African racism is not a domestic issue, then
American racism also is not a domestic issue.*

*Many of you have been led to believe that the
much publicized, recently passed civil-rights bill is
a sign that America is making a sincere effort to
correct the injustices we have suffered there. This
propaganda maneuver is part of her deceit and*

trickery to keep the African nations from condemning her racist practices before the United Nations, as you are now doing as regards the same practices of South Africa.

The United States Supreme Court passed a law ten years ago making America's segregated school system illegal. But the federal government has yet to enforce this law even in the North. If the federal government cannot enforce the law of the highest court in the land when it comes to nothing but equal rights to education for African-Americans, how can anyone be so naive as to think all the additional laws brought into being by the civil-rights bill will be enforced?

These are nothing but tricks of the century's leading neo-colonialist power. Surely, our intellectually mature African brothers will not fall for this trickery.

The Organization of Afro-American Unity, in cooperation with a coalition of other Negro leaders and organizations, has decided to elevate our freedom struggle above the domestic level of civil rights. We intend to "internationalize" it by placing it at the level of human rights. Our freedom struggle for human dignity is no longer confined to the domestic jurisdiction of the United States government.

We beseech the independent African states to help us bring our problem before the United Nations, on the grounds that the United States government is morally incapable of protecting the lives and the property of 22 million African-Americans. And on the grounds that our deteriorating plight is definitely becoming a threat to world peace.

Out of frustration and hopelessness our young people have reached the point of no return. We no *longer endorse patience and turning-the-other-cheek. We assert the right of self defense by whatever means necessary, and reserve the right of maximum retaliation against our racist oppressors, no matter what the odds against us are.*

From here on in, if we must die anyway, we will die fighting back and we will not die alone. We intend to see that our racist oppressors also get a taste of death.

We are well aware that our future efforts to defend ourselves by retaliating—by meeting violence with violence, eye for eye and tooth for tooth —could create the type of racial conflict in America that could easily escalate into a violent, world-wide, bloody race war.

In the interests of world peace and security, we beseech the heads of the independent African states to recommend an immediate investigation into our problem by the United Nations Commission on Human Rights.

If this humble plea that I am voicing at this conference is not properly worded, then let our elder brothers, who know the legal language, come to our aid and word our plea in the proper language necessary for it to be heard.

One last word, my beloved brothers at this African summits

"No one knows the master better than his servant." We have been servants in American for over 300 years. We have a thorough, inside knowledge of this man who calls himself "Uncle Sam." Therefore, you must heed our warning: Don't escape from European colonialism only to become even more enslaved by deceitful, "friendly" American dollarism.

May allah's blessings of good health and wisdom be upon you all.

Signed, Malcolm X, Chairman
Organization of Afro-American Unity

The African heads of States received the document and that was the end of the matter. Not a single state executive instructed his ambassador to bring the Negro question to the floor of the United Nations. Yet an ever-dreaming Malcolm returned home and issued this incredible statement:

"Well, one of the main objectives of the OAAU is to join the civil-rights struggle and lift it above civil rights to the level of human rights. As long as our people wage a struggle for freedom and label it civil rights, it means that we are under the domestic jurisdiction of Uncle Sam continually, and no outside nation can make any effort whatsoever to help us. As soon as we lift it above civil rights to the level of human rights, the problem becomes internationalized; all of those who belong to the United Nations automatically can take sides with us and help us in condemming, at least charging, Uncle Sam with violation of our human rights."

The clear implication was that the United Nations would debate the American race question if we would only substitute "human rights" for "civil rights." It was a shoddy performance; for years it had been abundantly evident that African States would not offend the American State Department. Once again, by establishing his Organization of Afro-American Unity, Malcolm had mistaken myth-rhetoric for a program. And it is significant that on the day after Malcolm presented his memorandum to the African heads of state Harlem erupted with the bloody riots of July 18, 1964.

There was yet a final myth: The notion—based on fact—that globally viewed the American Negro is part of the world's non-white majority. Malcolm was much inclined toward this myth; indeed it was the philosophical base of Malcolm's attempts to "internationalize the American black man's struggle." A month after he broke from Elijah Muhammad Malcolm spoke before the Militant Labor Forum, a discussion group sponsored by a socialist weekly, *The Militant*. The audience was overwhelmingly white, liberal and democratic; they were, for the most part, hostile to Malcolm. The Black Muslim apostate began his talk by addressing "Ladies and gentlemen, friends and enemies." Then, halfway through the speech, he said this:

"Among the so-called Negroes in this country, as a rule the civil-rights groups, those who believe in civil rights, spend most of their time trying to prove they are Americans. Their thinking is usually domestic, confined to the boundaries of America, and they always look upon themselves as a minority. When they look upon themselves upon the American stage, the American stage is a white stage. So a black man standing on that stage in America automatically is in the minority. He is the underdog, and in his struggle he always uses an approach that is a begging, hat-in-hand, compromising approach.

"Whereas the other segment or section in America, known as the black nationalists, are more interested in human rights than they are in civil rights. And they place more stress on human rights than they do on civil rights. The difference between the thinking and the scope of the Negroes who are involved in the civil-rights struggle and those who are involved in the human-rights struggle is that those so-called Negroes involved in the human-rights struggle don't look upon themselves as Americans.

"They look upon themselves as a part of dark mankind. They see the whole struggle not within the confines of the American stage, but they look upon the struggle on the world stage. And, in the world context, they see that the dark man out-numbers the white man. On the world stage the white man is just a microscopic minority."

As Malcolm well knew, only a brave man indeed would instruct the militant youths of Harlem to be of good cheer and rejoice in the knowledge that they are part of the world's non-white majority. As the Bandung Conference of the late fifties proved decisively, there is no possibility of organizing the world's non-white majority into an effective tool of liberation.

The only hope, then, for the American black man lay here at home. The black man must manipulate the American machinery—by nonviolence or by violence—and cause it to work in his behalf. This is what the militant black power advocates were brooding and plotting about. Indeed as Malcolm was traveling in Kenya he encountered John Lewis and Donald Harris, two SNCC Ambassadors who were trekking through black Africa in search of support in the United Nations. They, too, were attempting to "internationalize" the Negro's strug-gle. Like Malcolm, they came home empty-handed. But after these ambassadors returned home they caucused with their fellow black militants. It is now clear that the decision was made to disrupt Ameri-can cities.

For reasons that have been explored at length in this chapter, Malcolm was never able to effect an alliance with the young black militants who were then plotting the crisis that is now upon the republic. His trip to Selma was arranged by SNCC people but no alliance resulted. The black power people would later raise Malcolm to sainthood but they would not work with him, nor let him work with them, in life.

THIRTEEN

MARTIN LUTHER KING AND BLACK POWER

The scene was a Miami Beach hotel early February, 1968. Some one hundred clergymen from across the nation had gathered there to assist Martin Luther King in his efforts to organize a poor peoples' march on Washington, D.C. With the lone exception of a white clergyman who pastors a church in the black ghetto of St. Louis, all of the ministers in attendance were black. King himself wore a button that read "Black Is Beautiful." The Martin King of this meeting was a totally different man from the flaming integrationist who had worked miracles in Montgomery, Birmingham and Selma with scores of white Protestant, Catholic and Jewish clergymen at his side. The times had forced Martin to embrace a modified form of black power.

The turning point had come during the summer and fall of 1964, in Selma, Alabama. King had mounted his Selma campaign with the aid of white liberals and young students from the Student Nonviolent Coordinating Committee. The black students marched with King but their hearts were not in the protest; some of them were jailed with Martin but—for them, that is—it was an empty gesture. They had seen too much, mourned the violent death of too many of their comrades to any longer believe that King's brand of nonviolent demonstration would produce meaningful results.

The students' attitude toward Martin was that of
any child who becomes convinced that his father is
senile. They were kind, loving, and—for the most
part—obedient; but they seized every opportunity
to let Martin know they felt he was wrong. The
divisive issue, of course, was Martin's insistence
that the conscience of white America could be
moved to action by nonviolent protest. Not only did
the black students doubt the good faith of white
America but they were hostile toward the white
liberals who came into the South as civil rights
volunteers as well.

The Selma march incurred the wrath of Sheriff
Jim Clarke who ordered his men to tear gas the
marchers. As the marchers scattered in search of
pure air many were chased by police and beaten to
the ground; scores were injured and even more,
including Martin King, were jailed. The entire
episode was shown on national television and the
nation recoiled in disbelief. As Martin languished in
jail his lieutenants sent out the call for his black and
white supporters from across the nation to converge
on Selma for a march to the state capital, Montgomery, Alabama.

Each night King's lieutenants held a rally in a
local church to drum up physical, financial, and
psychological support for the march. The clue to
what the young students involved were thinking
lies in the fact that two SNCC members quietly
invited Malcolm X who had just returned from
Africa to speak. As I will discuss in the following
chapter, there was more to that move than met the
public eye.

The police brutality at Selma had confirmed the
students' dire prophecies. And the sight of scores of
black men and women falling to the ground,

curling up fetus-like, as white policemen beat them with clubs caused many people to wonder if this type of nonviolence was not itself immoral. "There is something morally wrong about allowing a man to beat you when you are in the right," a Los Angeles minister remarked to me at the time. "The good man must strike back and chastise the evildoers (the police.)"

Martin's followers did not strike back. The people rose from the ground, Martin emerged from jail, and together they led some fifty thousand blacks and whites on the sixty-mile trek to Montgomery. More, the Selma police brutality caused the Congress to pass the comprehensive voting rights bill of 1965. As a technical and legal matter all American Negroes finally had the franchise. But, significantly enough, the Selma-Montgomery march marked the end of the nonviolent civil rights era that began in Montgomery ten years earlier and catapulted Martin Luther King, Jr. into national prominence.

Two things had happened: Negroes had grown weary of being beaten and jailed for attempting to exert their constitutional rights; and the unprecedented civil rights gains that were recorded failed to sift down to the black masses, particularly in the northern ghetto.

It was no accident, then, that Martin Luther King shifted both his target and his goals. He elected to improve the economic plight of the ghetto masses and Chicago was selected as the target city. By the time Martin made the decision to move against Chicago it was abundantly clear that the ghetto was the new center of racial concern. Watts had exploded into what was then the worst racial rampage in the nation's history; at least two score other cities also belched flames during the fiery and bloody summer of 1965.

Garbed in blue denims to reflect his oneness with the poor Martin King moved into a Chicago apartment and began hanging out on the street corners with the oppressed and disillusioned black men whose fury imploded into violence. That was a new Martin—the man who played pool and drank beer with the hustlers. For the first time he understood that integrated bathrooms and restaurants were totally irrelevant to the lives of blacks trapped in the gateless poverty of the northern ghetto. He also finally understood why nonviolence was becoming increasingly unacceptable.

On the Monday after the Watts rebellion Martin King came to Los Angeles and convened some fifty black spokesmen. "What caused Watts to explode?" Martin asked us. We gave him a list of complaints running from joblessness, to rats, to hopelessness. I realized then that Martin did not fully understand in his guts the madness induced by ghetto life. Few of the middle-class blacks who attended that meeting understood it. In my brief statement to the group I quoted a line from my book, *The Negro Revolt*, "If you find a Negro who is not schizoid he is crazy." The flip nature of the comment aside, the serious message I was attempting to convey was that the American experience, particularly in the ghetto, is designed to drive black people insane. Several months later, in Chicago, Martin came to understand what I meant:

To make good his identity with the black ghetto dwellers of Chicago, Martin packed up his family and moved into a rundown Chicago apartment building. After a month there Martin noticed a chilling change in his children; they became sullen and hostile; they would not obey. His son became outright defiant. With no place to play, being constantly surrounded by hopelessness and despair, the King child absorbed the syndrome of the ghetto. It was only a matter of time before they too would begin throwing bricks and fashioning Molotov cocktails. The children were shipped back home to the fresh air of black middle-class America.

The King children had the money to get out of the ghetto; they had a safe and secure home of grandparents as a refuge. The real ghetto dweller had no such escape; he was there with the core of the problem. In an unusual personal statement Martin wrote about his long nights of debate with those who felt that violence was the only solution for the ghetto dweller: "Over cups of coffee in my apartment in Chicago, I have often talked late at night and over into the small hours of the morning with proponents of Black Power who argued passionately about the validity of violence and riots. They don't quote Gandhi or Tolstoy. Their Bible is Frantz Fanon's *The Wretched of the Earth*. This black psychiatrist from Martinique, who went to Algeria to work with the National Liberation Front in its fight against the French, argues in his book— a well-written book, incidentally, with many penetrating insights—that violence is a psychologically healthy and tactically sound method for the oppressed. And so, realizing that they are a part of that vast company of the "wretched of the earth," these young American Negroes, who are predominantly involved in the Black Power movement, often quote Fanon's belief that violence is the only thing that will bring about liberation. As they say, "Sing us no songs of nonviolence, sing us no songs of progress, for nonviolence and progress belong to middle-class Negroes and whites and we are not interested in you."

Nor was that all; black power advocates chose the Chicago Campaign as an opportunity to openly attack their father-mentor. It was as if one's only begotten son had plunged the dagger in his father's back. I can feel the tears in Martin's soul as he described what transpired:

"Unfortunately, when hope diminishes, the hate is often turned most bitterly toward those who originally built up the hope. In all the speaking that I have done in the United Staes before varied audiences, including some hostile whites, the only time that I have been booed was one night in a Chicago mass meeting by some young members of the Black Power movement. I went home that night with an ugly feeling. Selfishly I thought of my sufferings and sacrifices over the last twelve years. Why would they boo one so close to them? But as I lay awake thinking, I finally came to myself, and I could not for the life of me have less than patience and understanding for those young people. For twelve years I, and others like me, had held out radiant promises of progress. I had preached to them about my dream. I had lectured to them about the not too distant day when they would have freedom, 'all, here and now.' I had urged them to have faith in America and in white society. Their hopes had soared. They were now booing because they felt that we were unable to deliver on our promises. They were booing because we had urged them to have faith in people who had too often proved to be unfaithful. They were now hostile because they were watching the dream that they had so readily accepted turn into a frustrating nightmare."

Even those of us who loved him completely and supported him totally were convinced that this was enough to dissuade Martin from his Chicago venture. But King persisted and encountered yet another reality of Northern ghetto life—the open opposition of entrenched black middle-class politicians who were inseparably allied with the white power structure.

Black Chicago is the political plantation of veteran Congressman William L. Dawson who is "H.N.I.C. (Head Nigger In Charge)" for Mayor Richard Daley. Dawson cracked the whip and a bevy of black clergymen raced on television to demand that Martin King get out of town. As a reporter who had been stationed in Chicago for almost ten years I knew what Martin did not know: By making a national public issue of the plight of Chicago's Negroes, Martin was on the verge of exposing not only a corrupt political system but the influence of the underworld in ghetto economic life as well. I was surprised, and honestly so, that Martin did not disappear into Lake Michigan, his feet encased in concrete. For this is the precise fate of those who threaten the nickle and dime numbers racket that rakes in millions of welfare client dollars each year; this is the precise fate of those who threaten the millions reaped each year by white underworld czars who peddle dope as an antidote for despair.

In Chicago, Martin Luther King found himself fighting *The System,* that powerful combination of exploitative merchants, corrupt politicians and amoral gangsters. These were the men who controlled ghetto life. They still do. Martin was reading the Bible and philosophy texts in search of guidance. He would have done better to read the words biographer Alex Haley was then writing about Malcolm X:

"Admitted to the underworld's fringes, sixteen-year-old Malcolm absorbed all he heard and saw. He swiftly built up a reputation for honesty by turning over every dollar due his boss ('I have always been intensely loyal'). By the age of 18, Malcolm was versatile "Big Red." He hired from four to six men variously plying dope, numbers, bootleg whiskey and diverse forms of hustling. Malcolm personally squired well-heeled white thrill-seekers to Harlem sin dens, and Negroes to white sin downtown. 'My best customers were preachers and social leaders, police and all kinds of big shots in the business of controlling other people's lives."

Taking on Bull Conner in Birmingham and Jim Clarke in Selma was one thing; taking on *The System* in Chicago was quite another. Poor Martin; no longer was his advisary a white bigot; rather it was that amalgam of unprincipled greed and political corruption that resulted in the indictment of Newark Police Commissioner Dominick Spina and the public expose of Senator Edward Long and Congressman Cornelius E. Gallagher. *Life* magazine exposed Senator Long's connection with the mob and just this year the people turned him out of office. Spina was indicted for his link to those who control gambling in riot-torn Newark. And as for Gallagher, not only does *Life* lay bare his alleged trafficking in an illegal cancer drug, but the magazine goes on to show why the New Jersey Congressman (from the suburbs of Newark) was of immense value to the mob:

"Among Gallagher's considerable attributes, so far as the mob was concerned, was his seat on the prestigious House Foreign Affairs Committee."

These disclosures may have been as much of a shock to the readers of *Life* as they were to Martin Luther King. But they are common knowledge to the man in the black ghetto. Mobsterism, death, as well as corruption in high places are his daily fare.

King's Chicago campaign, then, was doomed from the onset. He made some modest gains through "Operation Breadbasket" which forced some companies to hire blacks, some merchants to lower their prices, and a few landlords to make necessary repairs. King's march into Cicero, the suburban gangland of Chicago, was a total disaster that errupted into almost unprecedented white violence.

Chicago was Martin's first, and last, campaign outside the South. It was his big effort to stave off the black violence then spreading across the republic; it was his final stand against black power. Chicago was a failure, not for Martin himself, but for his Christian, nonviolent attack upon complex socio-economic problems. Chicago was final evidence that *The System* that controls the ghetto would not yield power to the nonviolent and the civilized. Only those who were willing to burn and loot had the power to get things done.

Back home in Atlanta, Martin closeted with his staff and brooded. They realized that Oswald Spengler's prediction that the American race problem would dissolve into a class problem had come true. Thus it was that Martin announced that he would lead a "poor peoples' march" on Washington.

The seed money for Martin Luther King's march on Washington came from white people but such were the times that Martin could not afford to have his white followers in on the planning. He would have lost his Negro followers had whites been allowed to participate. More, Martin was under incredible pressure from both blacks and whites who argued that it was no longer possible to stage a nonviolent march in America.

Martin was determined to stage the Washington march. He assembled the black clergy from across the nation in Miami in the full faith that they not only would support his march but that, in the process, they would inherit the power in the ghetto and thus displace the black power militants who openly advocated burning the community down.

Martin Luther King was a dreamer. His assumption that black clergymen could take power in the ghettos was, by far, the most ethereal dream he ever entertained. Black power militants reserve their most passionate hate for the black Christian church. But in a blatant compromise with reality Martin King went "black." He dressed in the overalls of the poor, he proudly displayed his "Black Is Beautiful" button, and he wrote a book in which he adopted a modified form of black power.

The black clergy assembled in Miami, voted to support Martin although even they pondered the wisdom of congregating so many black and poor people in the nation's capital. By then Martin's innards were twisted in a double knot; his faith in Christians had been deeply shaken by the behavior of the white Protestants and Catholics in Chicago; now Martin's closest black supporters and fellow clergymen were doubting that an assemblage of black protesters ever again could remain nonviolent.

Martin Luther King needed a proving ground, an arena in which he could stage a successful nonviolent march and at the same time assume a modified black power stance that would reclaim the black

militants who had defected after marching with
Martin dozens of times only to drink the bitter
water of white brutality.

Then came a Macedonian call from Memphis,
Tennessee. The garbage workers, ninety-nine percent of whom were black, were in trouble and on
strike. Memphis was the proving ground Martin
needed to revalidate his credentials to march on
Washington. He answered the call to come to
Memphis. He would not leave that Southern town
alive.

FOURTEEN

PREACH WHAT YOU PRACTICE OR PRACTICE WHAT YOU PREACH

"No one will accept anything relating to me but my old hate and violence image," Malcolm said to Alex Haley a month before he was murdered. "The so-called 'moderate' civil rights organizations regard me as 'too militant' and the so-called 'militant' organizations avoid me as 'too moderate.' They won't let me turn the corner!"

What corner was Malcolm attempting to negotiate? Indeed, did Malcolm himself know where he was going?

These two questions have haunted students of Malcolm for four years. His last speeches provide some hints but no complete answers. Perhaps those who were closely associated with him during his last fifty weeks on earth know the full truth; I doubt it. Malcolm never completely trusted anyone. My own conviction is that Malcolm did not share the all of his thinking, the all of his African-Asian alliances, with anyone—not even his wife. A good deal of dust has now settled over Malcolm's grave and I have encountered a few people who are now willing to disclose more information than that which came to the fore immediately after the assassination. I believe I now know what happened to Malcolm X; I think I can detail the corner he was attempting to turn:

Malcolm X embraced yet another conviction, a

dogma, and he formed international alliances with individuals and groups who were eager to assist him in his efforts to convert the American Negro to this dogma. Malcolm was cut down before his program was clearly defined; but even if he had lived I doubt that his private problems—lack of money and animus toward Elijah Muhammad— would have left him with enough physical and mental energy to carry out the program he had in mind.

THE NEW CONVICTION: Malcolm X was always a man of deep conviction and passionate commitment. As Big Red, the pimp and dope peddler, Malcolm is still a legend in Harlem. Nobody— but nobody—outpimped and outpeddled Big Red; and he did it with a flourish. As a Black Muslim evangelist, Minister Malcolm X was the best disciple Elijah Muhammad ever had, the most respected preacher Elijah will ever have; and he did it with a flourish.

During the weeks and months of his suspension by Elijah, Malcolm pondered and brooded; he was in search of a new philosophy, of a way to finance the organization he would build upon that philosophy. It never occurred to Malcolm simply to get a job and go to work as common men do. Malcolm was entranced by himself as a leader and platform person. Emotionally he could never abandon that role.

Malcolm's first move was to establish his Muslim Mosque, Inc. Although Malcolm announced the religious movement would be an umbrella organization for blacks of all religious faiths, Muslim Mosque, Inc. was little more than The Nation of Islam all over again, with Malcolm, instead of Elijah, as the spiritual leader. The initial membership was com-

prised of some fifty persons who defected from
Elijah to follow Malcolm. Malcolm's thinking had
not basically changed; he was still in the religious "bag." I agree with other writers who suggest that Malcolm made the trip to Mecca to give
himself final authentication as a religious—Moslem
—leader. But even before he left for Mecca, Malcolm realized that he had made a false start. Not
only were his Moslem—or Muslim—teachings totally irrelevant to the blood and fire that were spreading over Harlem but they ceased to answer the
questions Malcolm's agile mind was forcing upon
him. This accounts—at least I suggest that it does—
for this shocking statement by Malcolm during his
transition period: "If I discover that I am caught up
in a religion that will not allow me to fight the
battle for black men, then I say to hell with that
religion!"

During the days after his severance from Elijah,
Malcolm faced himself and realized that his ultimate commitment was not to Islam; it was to
American blacks. He further realized that he could
not prevail so long as he stood on a religious—
Moslem—platform. From those who were closely
allied with him I know that Malcolm had begun to
think in terms of political and economic solutions to
the Negro problem. He said as much during his
Cleveland speech on April 3, 1964, a month after he
left the Black Muslim movement. Malcolm said the
Negro would achieve full freedom in America
either by the ballot or the bullet. That is hardly the
thinking of a man whose ultimate commitment is to
Islam.

But the deepest change that was occurring within
Malcolm had to do with economic philosophy. Malcolm X became convinced that the black man's

problem could not be solved within the framework of American capitalism as it now functions. Malcolm's thoughts almost surfaced during an interview with Carlos E. Russell three weeks after he formed the Muslim Mosque, Inc. Russell asked Malcolm why he and other Negro leaders did not advocate socialism. Malcolm replied:

"Why speak of it! If you want someone to drink from a bottle, you never put the skull and crossbones on the label, for they won't drink. The same is true there."

Two weeks following this interview Malcolm enplaned for Mecca and Africa. Malcolm's autobiography details his experiences in Mecca but we have only a skimpy account of Malcolm's experiences in Africa. Malcolm kept detailed notes but, as he himself said, he kept his diary a secret since it was to be the basis of a new book he intended to write. Malcolm was royally received by several heads of state and he gives a minute account of these receptions in his autobiography. But nothing is said of the private African contacts that so clearly affected his thinking.

Powerful African leaders privately told Malcolm that his religious approach was nonsensical. They bluntly advised him to embrace the "economic" revolution that was sweeping the world. Of particular significance were Malcolm's experiences with a group of American Negroes living in Ghana. Malcolm worked with them as they organized the Organization of African Unity. Kwame Nkrumah, an avowed socialist, was then the Ghanian head of state and it is not accidental that Malcolm forged a close friendship with the then Algerian ambassador to Ghana whom Malcolm called "a true revolutionary in the true sense of the word."

When Malcolm X returned home to New York on May 21, 1964, he was a changed man. Reporters were so obsessed with his Mecca induced discovery that not all white men were devils that they failed to probe the truly significant shift in Malcolm's thought. The shift was economic, not ethnic. But Malcolm's new thinking did surface a week later when Malcolm once again spoke before the Militant Labor Forum. This is what he said:

"They say travel broadens your scope, and recently I've had an opportunity to do a lot of it in the Middle East and Africa. While I was traveling I noticed that most of the countries that have recently emerged into independence have turned away from the so-called capitalistic system in the direction of socialism. So out of curiosity, I can't resist the temptation to do a little investigating wherever that particular philosophy happens to be in existence or an attempt is being made to bring it into existence.

"It's impossible for a chicken to produce a duck egg—even though they both belong to the same family of fowl. A chicken just doesn't have it within its system to produce a duck egg. It can't do it. It can only produce according to what that particular system was constructed to produce. The system in this country cannot produce freedom for an Afro-American. It is impossible for this system, this economic system, this political system, this social system, this system, period. It's impossible for this system, as it stands, to produce freedom right now for the black man in this country.

"And if ever a chicken did produce a duck egg, I'm quite sure you would say it was certainly a revolutionary chicken!"

Following the speech a member of the forum

asked Malcolm to spell out his personal economic philosophy. Malcolm replied:

"I don't know. But I'm flexible—As was stated earlier, all of the countries that are emerging today from under the shackles of colonialism are turning toward socialism. I don't think it's an accident. Most of the countries that were colonial powers were capitalist countries, and the last bulwark of capitalism today is America. It's impossible for a white person to believe in capitalism and not believe in racism. You can't have capitalism without racism. And if you find one and you happen to get that person into a conversation and they have a philosophy that makes you sure they don't have this racism in their outlook, usually they're socialists or their political philosophy is socialism."

During his stay in Mecca and Africa Malcolm's organization, the Muslim Mosque, Inc., all but atrophied. This did not disturb Malcolm for he had returned home with a new philosophy and was bent upon founding yet a new organization. Within a matter of days Malcolm announced the formation of the Organization of Afro-American Unity, the sister organization of the Organization of African Unity he had helped midwife while in Ghana. It was at this point that the CIA began to take an active interest in Malcolm's activities.

Six weeks after announcing the formation of his new movement, the Organization of Afro-American Unity, Malcolm quit the United States for an eighteen week visit to the Middle East and Africa. Malcolm quit America just as the militant blacks were rioting in Rochester, Brooklyn, Harlem, Philadelphia and a score of other cities. He quit the black ghetto for black Africa just as a congress of black intellectuals was issuing a statement to the effect that Malcolm was the only black leader who had the confidence of the black masses; that Martin Luther King had the confidence of the Negro middle class but that if King wished to survive as leader he must move toward Malcolm X.

There is a still unexplained and odd aspect of Malcolm's last trip to Africa. Malcolm goes to great lengths in his autobiography to tell us that he was broke. He borrowed the money for his Mecca-Africa trip from his sister, Ella Collins. But by mid-July Malcolm had somehow gathered sufficient funds to (1) take an eighteen week journey through the Middle East and Africa; (2) provide for his family while he was away; (3) maintain his OAAU office and staff in Harlem's Theresa Hotel. Where did the money come from?

New evidence suggests that Malcolm found money sources in Africa. As early as 1960 Ghana was the haven for black African revolutionaries who were mapping plans to overthrow the colonial governments in their several countries. In my book *The Reluctant African,* I detailed these activities and suggested that Algeria was the conduit through which "eastern" money reached these revolutionaries in Ghana. But, having seen the manner in which African revolutionaires were supported, I doubt that his "backers" provided him with a good deal of cash money. He probably got enough money to sustain his family and organization in New York. As for the trip, Malcolm was probably given air tickets and spending money; he was the guest of the various countries he visited. The state paid his bills.

Malcolm's central problem—and this is why he remained in Africa three times longer than he had planned to—was his inability to convince his

"backers" that the American black man was ready
for revolution. They hosted him royally and listened to his case but there was nothing in the file
they had compiled on Malcolm to convince these
African revolutionaries that Malcolm and his
OAAU merited a major outlay of money. But Malcolm was able to establish a conduit through which
funds would be made available once he demon-
strated what he and his organization could accomplish in America. Alas, the African revolutionaries
were more interested in dealing with the black
militants who set off the urban flames that belched
while Malcolm merely talked. Even so Malcolm X
forged a major link with Middle East and African
revolutionaries while he was in Nkrumah's Ghana.
By then the CIA was following Malcolm's every
move; agents were aboard every flight he took, other
agents watched his hotels and even kept him under
surveillance during meal time.

James Farmer, the former Director of CORE,
was in Ghana shortly after Malcolm left. A top
politician there told Farmer that Malcolm was
marked for assassination. What the politician didn't
tell Farmer was that Nkrumah would soon be
overthrown with the aid of the CIA.

Early in November Malcolm returned home. His
mission had been a failure in that he did not get the
immediate financial support he needed. He did get
commitments based upon his ability to perform;
but his much neglected OAAU was without organizational muscle. It is also doubtful that those devoted followers who still gathered with Malcolm in
the OAAU office were as strongly committed to
world socialism as Malcolm was. George Breitman
has arranged Malcolm's last speeches in a chronolog-

ical order that eliminates all doubt as to what corner Malcolm was turning.

On November 23, 1964—en route home from Africa—Malcolm stopped off in Paris for a speech sponsored by the socialist magazine *Presence Africaine*. Malcolm unleashed a scathing attack on American left wingers who "call themselves Marxists, who claim to be enemies of the system, but who (were) on their hands and knees working for Johnson's election."

Less than a month later Malcolm gave this appraisal of independent African states before a black audience in New York:

"Almost every one of the countries that has gotten independence has devised some kind of socialistic system, and this is no accident. This is another reason why I say that you and I here in America—who are looking for a job, who are looking for better housing, looking for a better education—before you start trying to be incorporated, or integrated, or disintegrated, into this capitalistic system, should look over there and find out what are the people who have gotten their freedom adopting to provide themselves with better housing and better education and better food and better clothing.

"None of them are adopting the capitalistic system because they realize they can't. You can't operate a capitalistic system unless you are vulturistic; you have to have someone else's blood to suck to be a capitalist. You show me a capitalist, I'll show you a bloodsucker. He cannot be anything but a bloodsucker if he's going to be a capitalist. He's got to get it from somewhere other than himself, and that's where he gets it—from somewhere or someone other than himself . . .

"There's one thing that Martin Luther King mentioned at the Armory the other night, which I thought was most significant. I hope he really understood what he was saying. He mentioned that while he was in some of those Scandinavian countries he saw no poverty. There was no unemployment, no poverty. Everyone was getting education, everyone had decent housing, decent whatever-they-needed-to-exist. But why did he mention those countries on his list as different?

"This is the richest country on earth and there's poverty, there's bad housing, there's slums, there's inferior education. And this is the richest country on earth. Now, you know, if those countries that are poor can come up with a solution to their problems so that there's no unemployment, then instead of you running downtown picketing city hall, you should stop and find out what they do over there to solve their problems. This is why the man doesn't want you and me to look beyond Harlem or beyond the shores of America. As long as you don't know what's happening on the outside, you'll be all messed up dealing with this man on the inside. I mean what they use to solve the problems is not capitalism. What they are using to solve their problem in Africa and Asia is not capitalism. So what you and I should do is find out what they are using to get rid of poverty and all the other negative characteristics of a rundown society."

Two weeks later during an interview with the newspaper *Young Socialist,* Malcolm commented:

"It is impossible for capitalism to survive, primarily because the system of capitalism needs some blood to suck. Capitalism used to be like an eagle, but now it's more like a vulture. It used to be strong enough to go and suck anybody's blood, whether they were strong or not. But now it has become more cowardly, like the vulture, and it can only suck the blood of the helpless. As the nations of the world free themselves, then capitalism has less victims, less to suck, and it becomes weaker and weaker. It's only a matter of time in my opinion before it will collapse completely."

And in his last formal lecture Malcolm told a Columbia University audience;

"We are living in an era of revolution, and the revolt of the American Negro is part of the rebellion against the oppression and colonialism which has characterized this era . . .

"It is incorrect to classify the revolt of the Negro as simply a racial conflict of black against white, or as a purely American problem. Rather, we are today seeing a global rebellion of the oppressed against the oppressor, the exploited against the exploiter."

The obvious question is why the American socialists and African revolutionaries didn't bail Malcolm out of his private financial difficulties? He was about to become the most exciting black spokesman they had had since the turn of the century. Yet they allowed him to all but starve and then to be murdered. Why?

One of Malcolm's closest and most trusted non-Muslim advisers has told me that Malcolm developed deep doubts about his socialist and African revolutionary "backers" during the last weeks of his life. This source, a man in position to know the details of Malcolm's private affairs, is convinced that Malcolm was on the verge of reneging on certain commitments he made in Africa.

Two things are clear: Malcolm never did trust the white Americans who comprise the socialist movement in this country; they never liked or trusted him. Secondly, the African revolutionaries sent Malcolm home, relatively speaking, empty-handed. Bluntly put, Malcolm was a brilliant polemicist but the world revolutionaries with whom he consorted in Africa openly doubted his ability to deliver. I watched the African revolutionaries administer the same treatment for the same reason to black South African exiles in 1960. More, not only did they doubt Malcolm but they well knew that for years the American Negro had resisted socialism and communism with a passion exhibited by no other group in the world.

In essence, then, Malcolm came home with a promise of help if he could muster a considerable socialist and revolutionary following among the black masses. Malcolm could not do this; he knew this. Alone, then, he was groping for ideas, grubbing for money.

The tragedy of Malcolm is even more pronounced in the light of new information indicating that Malcolm had a large sum of money just beyond his grasp at the time of his assassination. This new information revolves around one, perhaps two, unpublisized trips Malcolm made to Switzerland in connection with bank business there. There are those, particularly members of Malcolm's family, who say that the trip (or trips) were made by Malcolm in the hope that he could expose secret bank accounts held by Elijah Muhammad. Other, and more believable, evidence suggests that Malcolm was involved in an escrow deal with certain African contacts. Malcolm X was clearly supported by the Ben Bella-Nkrumah axis; Ben Bella was then ruler of Algeria and Nkrumah was the master of Ghana. It follows, then, that the enemies of these two African heads of state were Malcolm's enemies.

One must pause, now, and remember the international history of the years 1964 and 1965. Both Ben Bella and Nkrumah were under scathing attack from the American State Department; they were viewed as Red China's strongest links to Africa. Both men returned America's ire; they seized every opportunity to label America as an "imperialist." And it was to Ben Bella and Nkrumah that Malcolm made his major plea for help; it was they who arranged for him to be an "observer" at the summit meeting of African heads of state; it was they who arranged his final, and lavish, eighteen-week visit to Africa.

But Ben Bella and Nkrumah exacted something in return; something more immediate and tangible than the gathering of the American black man into the arms of world socialism.

The CIA was operating overtime in both Ghana and Algeria. The Bay of Pigs incident of 1963 was clear evidence that the CIA was obviously in the business of overthrowing socialist- and communist-leaning governments. Both Ben Bella and Nkrumah presided over restless armies whose officers were itching for coups that would bring them to power. These army men were known to be in touch with the CIA.

When Malcolm returned home from Africa via Switzerland, then, his assignment was curt: Rally the American black man and bring pressure against the American government to end its CIA activities in both Algeria and Ghana.

It was a neat "tit for tat" indeed. Malcolm wanted their help in his efforts to get the American blacks' problem thrashed out in the United Nations; they wanted Malcolm's help in rallying American blacks against the State Department's interference in Algerian and Ghanian affairs.

Malcolm X returned home to face a spate of personal problems that rendered him incapable of logically carrying out any program. First off the courts ruled that Elijah Muhammad's Black Muslims were the legal owners of the home Malcolm and his wife had occupied for several years. Malcolm was ordered to vacate the manse. Secondly, Malcolm came under an intensive investigation by the Internal Revenue Service. So ruthless was the investigation that agents demanded that Malcolm pay income tax on the advance received from his autobiography although they knew full well that Malcolm never received the money, that he had ordered the fee paid directly to Elijah Muhammad. (Malcolm was still with the Black Muslim movement when he contracted to do the book.) Malcolm's organization, the OAAU, was in shambles; and if one is to accept statements issued by his sister, Mrs. Ella Collins, Malcolm's wife was seriously considering divorcing him.

In addition to reading Haley's final versions of the autobiography Malcolm spent his last weeks fulfilling minor speaking engagements and making yet unexplained trips across the nation. At about the same time Malcolm announced that he was a marked man, that the Black Muslims were out to kill him. There was some evidence to support Malcolm's claim.

Death threats were telephoned to both Malcolm's home and office. Hardly a day passed that New York newspapers did not receive an anonymous call from someone saying they were going to kill Malcolm. Malcolm's schedule prevented him from delivering a speech in Boston; he sent an OAAU assistant instead. The car bearing the assistant was blocked in Boston's East Tunnel by a carload of Black Muslims. The Muslims allegedly carried knives and dispersed only after the pro-Malcolm forces bared shotguns. In yet another incident Malcolm's private phone was disconnected for "vacation" after the telephone company received a call from a mysterious "Mrs. Small." The most chilling incidents occurred during a trip Malcolm made to Los Angeles and Chicago late in January, 1965, less than a month before he was assassinated.

Malcolm landed in Los Angeles at three o'clock on the afternoon of January 28 aboard TWA's flight No. 9 from New York. According to Alex Haley, a special police intelligence squad watched as Malcolm was greeted by two friends, Edward Bradley and Allen Jamal, and was driven to the Statler-Hilton Hotel in downtown Los Angeles. The hotel was surrounded by Black Muslims. Despite the ominous threat, Malcolm's friends drove him to the homes of two of Elijah's former secretaries who had accused the Black Muslim leader of adultery with them. More, Malcolm and his friends drove the former secretaries to the law office of Gladys Towles Root, the flamboyant attorney, where they made accusations against Muhammad.

Malcolm and his friends were constantly followed by the Black Muslims. One Black Muslim woman told me her husband was called out of bed to participate in the harassment of Malcolm. Malcolm's stay in Los Angeles was climaxed by a hair-rising ride to the airport during which Malcolm frightened off the Black Muslims who were chasing him down the freeway by poking a walking cane through his car window and making his tormentors believe it was a shotgun.

Malcolm flew from Los Angeles to Chicago where the identical scene was reenacted: Black Muslims invaded the lobby of his hotel and surrounded the television studio as Malcolm taped an interview with Irv Kupcinet. Following the interview, and with Black Muslims still following him, Malcolm sped to O'Hare International Airport and enplaned for New York.

Let us pause for a moment and review the Los Angeles-Chicago trip. Why did Malcolm make this journey?

Granted, Malcolm could not resist an opportunity to appear on television; but this does not explain his journey to be with Irv Kupcinet. Having been on the "Kup Show" four times (one of them with Malcolm), I know the show does not pay even expense money for its guests. And Malcolm was then in dire straits. Even if Malcolm had been willing to deplete what grocery money he had to fly to Chicago for television exposure, why the trip to Los Angeles?

A reassembling of the facts will provide the answer:

Late in 1962 Malcolm came to believe the "adulterer" rumors he had been hearing about Muhammad for several years. He sought counsel with Elijah's son, Wallace, who confirmed the rumors but advised Malcolm that Elijah Muhammad would resent efforts to help clear the issue. Malcolm then broke the rules which forbade him to contact a Muslim under suspension or ousted from the movement. He tracked down and talked to the two secretaries in question. Not only did they confirm that Elijah fathered their children but they went on to tell Malcolm that Elijah considered him his best minister but one that would soon turn against Elijah and become "dangerous."

Malcolm arranged a meeting with Muhammad and confronted his spiritual leader with the charges the secretaries had made. Malcolm did not raise questions about Elijah's reported attitude toward him. As I have already discussed, Elijah not only admitted the extramarital intimacies but he justified them by saying he, Muhammad, must fulfill the prophecy—and the polygamous acts—of Old Testament heroes.

On July 3, 1963, the two secretaries told the press they were filing paternity suits against Elijah Muhammad. But the two women had only their word as evidence. Malcolm X was the only person who had heard Elijah's confession from his own lips. For eighteen months—including the weeks of his suspension—Malcolm had kept silent about the matter.

Only after he became convinced that the Black Muslims were out to kill him did Malcolm decide to make a public statement. He came to Los Angeles, then, to assist the two former secretaries in their suit against Muhammad. Every evidence is that he made the trip out of moral loyalty, at his own expense.

Malcolm also intended to use his visit to Los Angeles as an opportunity to organize a California branch of his OAAU. Several former L. A. Black Muslims had indicated they would join with Malcolm and he had planned to meet with them. So complete and ominous was the Black Muslims' surveillance, however, that Malcolm abandoned plans for the meeting and left town. The stopover in Chicago was nothing more than a part of the return trip to New York.

Only a few days after he arrived back in New

York, Malcolm enplaned for Selma, Alabama, where he frightened the daylights out of jailed Martin Luther King's lieutenants. He then flew to France where he was scheduled to address the Congress of African Students. The French allowed Malcolm to enter the country but they forbade him to speak. He was asked to leave the country and to consider himself "forever an undesirable person." Malcolm left France; he stopped over in London for a BBC-TV program and then flew home to discover that the final Appellate Court order had been issued for him and his family to vacate the East Elmhurst home that had been adjudged the rightful property of the Black Muslims.

It was the Malcolm X of this final period who troubled even his most loyal supporters. Some critics were unkind enough to label him a "con man," while those who loved him felt he had cracked under the strain, that he was mentally ill.

My own view is that Malcolm, like all Gaul, was divided into three parts. There was the Malcolm X who had made a private commitment to those who had a vendetta against Elijah Muhammad; there was the Malcolm who had made international commitments to major Algerian and Ghanian figures—and he was embarrassed because he could not immediately deliver on those commitments. Then there was the Malcolm who was struggling to keep his private finances and personal organization in order.

I know what Malcolm wanted to do: His dream was to implement his "Billy Graham" stance as the evangelist of international black nationalism; he wanted to move about the earth demanding justice for the black American and arousing support for the revolutionary regimes in Africa—particularly in

Algeria and Ghana. Most of all Malcolm was determined to somehow expose American racism to world view on the floor of the United Nations.

Had Malcolm lived, and had he been able to solve his private problems, I think he would have emerged as the major black American figure of the century. This would certainly have come to pass had Ben Bella and Nkrumah survived along with Malcolm. But it was not to be. Too many powerful national and international forces were against these three men.

Malcolm returned home from London on February 13, 1965, to begin the last tormented week of his life. The same week Algerian Army strongman Houari Boumedienne announced that his troops would "deal with Algeria's enemies"; twelve weeks later Houari Boumedienne deposed Ben Bella. The revolutionary Ben Bella simply vanished, never to be seen again. Nine months later Nkrumah was deposed from power while en route to Peking. He now languishes under lavish house arrest in nearby Guinea.

Malcolm was totally convinced that America was a racist state that escaped world criticism by shrewd public relations and dollar diplomacy. His anger was deepened by his conviction that not only was America racist but that the nation collectively lied about it.

"One thing I am determined to do, Lomax," he once said to me, "is to make America practice what it preaches or preach what it practices."

But assassins' bullets soon were to practice what those who wished Malcolm dead had been preaching.

FIFTEEN

FROM MEMPHIS TO THE MOUNTAINTOP

Black violence was a bitter thought for Martin Luther King, Jr. to entertain. Yet it was real, present, and uncompromising. What had started out as an incredible attempt to bring about major social change through nonviolent methods was transmuted into violence, burnings, looting, and riots in every major American city. Not that King's forces turned toward violence—far from it. Rather those black masses who reaped so little of King's civil rights harvest lost faith in both King and the American republic. It was a bitter and difficult moment for a man who had built a movement upon the firm faith that white America had a conscience, that this conscience could be changed through nonviolent struggle and suffering.

As magnificent as his dream was, Martin Luther King's philosophy was fundamentally flawed from the onset. Power, as Lord Acton remarked, yields only to power, and even then not without a struggle. History simply does not support King's faith in the ultimate goodness of men, black or white. Rather, history, without a single exception, teaches that freedom belongs to those who have the power to take it. King understood this; but he translated "power" as "redemptive love and suffering"—a super Christian concept which meant everything to the ethical philosopher, but nothing to the white bigot. Indeed the men King came up against viewed the brutality they visited upon him and his followers as not only a civic responsibility but the will of God as well.

The amazing thing is that King's tactic worked as well as it did. By marching, singing, praying and suffering, Martin Luther King let America out of the prison of legal segregation. Only after the prison walls fell was it fully laid bare that the inmates of segregation had been maimed for life. Their tortured souls could be heard groaning in agony and despair from Mississippi to Cleveland's Hough, from Georgia to Watts, from Alabama to Harlem. King—admittedly with much help—had opened the door but the newly freed men were too crippled by experience to walk in. The black masses were but a disturbing statistic. Comparatively speaking, their plight was worse at the time of his death than it was when he first entered the civil rights arena. The entire American economic wagon had rumbled forward but the gap between the front and back wheels—the whites and the blacks—had grown wider, not narrowed.

The long hot summers had rendered it all but impossible for large numbers of blacks to gather, except for religious and middle class affairs, without the real possibility of violence and rioting. More painful to Martin Luther King was the undeniable fact that violence paid off. As killings, burning and looting spread from city to city, the white power structure responded with reforms King never could have gotten through nonviolent supplication. In the wake of Martin's death Congress passed the national open housing law, the very goal King sought during his violence-scarred march through Cicero, Illinois.

The Martin who marched on Memphis was a

driven man. More than any other black American he bypassed several excellent opportunities to quit the forefront of the civil rights movement, to go in another direction. A hundred pulpits were his for the asking; there was not a single major university that did not have a vacant chair waiting for Martin Luther King to take occupancy. No one would have blamed him for accepting one of those offers; he did not have to die by an assassin's bullet. But he elected to risk death in Memphis.

King's determination to stage a poor people's march on Washington cost him the support of some of his best allies and most brilliant tacticians—notably Bayard Rustin who had choreographed the magnificent March On Washington in 1963. Rustin took to the floor of the Miami meeting called by King and bluntly told the black clergymen assembled that Martin no longer had the power to lead such a prolonged nonviolent protest. Rustin flatly refused to direct the protest march and then called a press conference to tell all the world that he was not associated with the project.

Little was said about it publicly but King had depleted his political capital in Washington. Most of his splendid victories had come when Washington—in the Eisenhower, Kennedy, and Johnson administrations—intervened to stop white brutality and enact legislation. But King's strong opposition to the Viet Nam war had alienated him from the Johnson administration. Many of the black clergy in attendance hesitated; they had different thoughts about Viet Nam and feared that by following King, the leader of the poor, they would be interpreted as following King the "dove" on Viet Nam. When the final vote was taken they all agreed to march with

King as he led the poor—ragged, tattered and on mules—to the seat of power.

Lurking in the foreground were the shadows of Stokely Carmichael and H. Rap Brown. Beginning in 1966, these two leaders of SNCC unleashed a black power doctrine which said, in essence, if it takes violence to change America, then there will be violence. During his last year Martin's stance was that of a tolerated "Uncle Tom" as he talked about the goodness of the Lord and the moral sensitivity of the American white man. The word was out that Carmichael and Brown were already laying plans to infiltrate the poor people's march and turn it into violence.

"We must not refrain from doing good," Martin intoned, "simply because outsiders might infiltrate our ranks and do evil." Yet no one knew better than Martin that if the Washington march erupted into violence the blame would be laid at his feet regardless of who set off the violence.

The world watched and America grew tense, then, as Martin moved into Memphis during the first of April, 1968, to march and champion the cause of the long suffering blacks of Memphis. The protest movement started out as a strike by Memphis garbage workers, almost all of whom are Negroes. But as the strike dragged on it involved the entire black community and the issues fissioned to include the problems of the black ghetto as a whole. Reflecting unprecedented organizing ability the Memphis movement enlisted some six thousand supporters to march in King's nonviolent march. But days before the march began there were unmistakable signs of trouble. Members of the gang known as The Invaders actually maneuvered their way onto the planning committee and openly proposed that the march be deliberately turned into a violent demonstration.

"Man," one of the Invaders preached, "you know, we want to get something done. I mean, all this stuff about marching downtown, all these bourgeoisie wanting to march downtown and get their pictures on national television doing their civil rights thing, man that's nothing. That ain't digging. That ain't going to help my brothers."

The Invaders mustered enough brass to ask a Memphis black clergyman to allow them to run off the formula for Molotov cocktails on the church mimeograph machine. The minister refused but the Invaders found an ally and the Molotov cocktail formulas were distributed.

At this point King's advance men arrived in town and pleaded their case for nonviolence before the Invader's tribunal.

"Man," snapped one of the tribunal, "if you expect honkies to get the message you got to break some windows."

Even so the moderates seemed to have carried the day and the indication was that The Invaders would either remain nonviolent or boycott the march. What actually happened on the day of the march is now under deep dispute. A secret federal government report that will be released about the time this book is published suggests that the Memphis police incited the violence—that they actually imported Highway Patrolmen from the neighboring state of Arkansas to deliberately foment trouble.

As the public record now stands, this is what occurred:

First off, black students at Hamilton High School raced out of the building to join the march. Riot ready white police attempted to force the young-

sters back into the school building. The students
filled the air with rocks and bottles; the police
responded with their billy clubs. When the turmoil
settled one Negro girl lay seriously injured. The
Invaders passed the word that the girl had been
killed by the police.

Meanwhile marchers were gathering at Clayborn
Temple Methodist Church, the staging ground for
the march. Middle class black women moved
through the marchers asking individuals if they
were "with the old folks or the young?" If they
were with the "young" then they were for violence
and were asked to quit the staging area. The Invaders left the march but they did not quit the
area. When Martin Luther King and his lieutenants
arrived at the staging area the Invaders and other
hostile black youth were gathered in a knot of
anger and hostility on the periphery of the marching column.

King and his lieutenants, arm in arm, had led the
marchers only a few yards when King was shoved
from behind by a group of jeering youths. Other
black militants raced ahead of the marchers and
began smashing store windows; picket signs turned
into weapons; looters began racing into alleys laden
with clothes and liquor. As police moved in with
tear gas and flailing billy clubs King's aides hustled
him into a white Pontiac and sped him to the safety
of his eighth floor suite at the white-owned Holiday Inn. The riot lasted three hours. The statistics:
sixty injured; two hundred and eighty arrested; one
dead.

Another casualty was the already weak hope that
Martin Luther King—or anybody else, for that matter—could ever lead a nonviolent black protest
march again. President Johnson took to television

three times that day to speak of "mindless violence" and the nation turned an even more anxious eye toward King's projected march of the poor on Washington.

But as the nation grew increasingly apprehensive about Martin's ability to lead a nonviolent march King became totally adamant. All of the fervor and dedication he had once invested in desegregating a Mississippi restroom was now committed to demonstrating that black Americans en masse could protest nonviolently.

A lesser man would have written off Memphis as the wrong march in the wrong city for the wrong reason. Not Martin.

"Nonviolence is on trial in Memphis," King lectured one of his staff workers. "It's either nonviolence or nonexistence." King was not just addressing himself to black Americans; the winner of the Nobel Peace Prize was talking to the world. *He who lives by the sword shall die by the sword. Either man brings an end to war or war will bring an end to man.*

The Martin Luther King I grew up with and loved and marched with had no moral alternative but to return to Memphis and prove his point.

And Martin did go back to Memphis. This time he assigned his advance men to mediate the turbulence, to make an amalgam of the black militants and the middle-class Negroes who wanted progress without violence. Martin's genius was his ability to work a miracle while dancing in the fire of certain defeat. He was on the verge of doing precisely that. All of the blacks, militants and moderates sat quietly in the Mason Street Temple as Martin King's supporters set the scene for the new march

that was to come, the nonviolent march that was to
vindicate King's career-long philosophy.

"It is important that nothing happens to Dr.
King," one minister shouted.

"Amen," the people answered.

"But for Dr. King," the clergyman continued,
"Memphis would be smoking right now!"

"Yes, Lord."

"King is the man, O Lord, that has been sent to
lead us out of the land of Egypt."

"Amen," the people answered.

Then, as loud applause and screaming "Amens"
resounded through the hall, Martin Luther King
moved to the lectern. He was tired, worried. Those
who were standing closest to him recall that his
eyes were faintly liquid. The opening line was a
familiar one; then he went on to be more prophetic
than even he knew:

"It is no longer a question of violence or nonviolence: it is a question of nonviolence or nonexistence."

By then the rain was tapping out a staccato tune
on the tin roof of Mason Temple.

"There was a bomb threat on my plane from
Atlanta," King told the shocked audience of several
hundred. "But it doesn't matter to me now. I've
been to the mountaintop; I've looked over and I
have seen the promised land. So I'm happy tonight.
I'm not worried about anything. I'm not fearing any
man. Mine eyes have seen the glory of the coming
of the Lord."

The meeting was adjourned with the understanding that they would all meet again the next night.
This meeting was but the first of a series of such
pep rallies designed to bring about total black unity
for a nonviolent demonstration. King and his aides

huddled late into the night in room 306 of the Lorraine Hotel, a Negro owned establishment to which King had moved after militant blacks complained that he was "living" downtown with the white folks."

As it always was with the *movement* meetings began all over again the next morning, Thursday.

"Dr. King really preached us a sermon," Hosea Williams, one of King's aides, recalled later. "He sensed that some of us had doubts about nonviolence. He said that the only hope of redeeming the soul of this nation was through nonviolence. He talked about the lives of Jesus and Gandhi, and he told us 'I have conquered the fear of death.' "

Martin Luther King had a dinner date to keep but he lingered over the balcony rail to talk with another staffer, Jessie Jackson, who was in the courtyard below.

"Doc," Jackson shouted up to King. "This is Ben Branch, the musician who is going to play for our rally tonight."

"Yes, yes," King answered back. "Branch is my man. Be sure to play 'Precious Lord,' Brother Branch. Be sure to play it pretty."

"It's chilly tonight, Dr. King," yet another aide standing behind Martin said. "You had better take along your coat."

"You are right," Martin said as he straightened up from the balcony rail. The cool Tennessee air was shattered by a shot from a high powered rifle.

Martin Luther King, Jr. had crossed over the mountaintop and away from this life.

SIXTEEN

BIG RED'S LAST WEEK

The last time I saw Malcolm X was on May 23, 1964, the night we debated at the Chicago Civic Opera House. Even as moderator Irv Kupcinet introduced Malcolm and me I could recognize Black Muslims—members of the Fruit of Islam—as they stationed themselves at strategic places in the cavernous auditorium. While we were in the back-stage dressing room Malcolm had told me the Black Muslims would be there, that they were out to kill him.

As a reporter I have been chased by the KKK in Mississippi, beaten in Little Rock, trapped in the Caribbean and Middle East wars. But never have I been quite as uneasy as I was that night as I walked to the lectern to give my opening speech. As I looked down from the stage I gazed into the eyes of John Ali, the man Malcolm had named as his archenemy in the Black Muslim inner circle. Not only were the Muslims angry with Malcolm because of his defection but John Ali had made public his anger towards me because I wrote in my book *When the Word is Given* that Ali was once an FBI agent.

I opened with a sarcastic attack on Malcolm because of his new beard. After pointing out that Malcolm had just returned from Mecca and Africa I asked if the beard was "philosophical as well as physical." But my real preoccupation was with John

Ali and the other Black Muslims as they deployed themselves throughout the hall. John returned my stare; we both knew what we had been through together. I was the only reporter to write the true story when the home John and Malcolm shared jointly was illegally invaded by police. It was John who arranged for me to first meet Malcolm. And John was there with Malcolm and me when the first issues of the sect's newspaper were published. More, John knew that my report of his FBI affiliation had not been maliciously written, that it was based upon persistent reports and information.

If Malcolm was afraid as he spoke he did not reflect it. I had polemically put him in a very awkward position. He had left the Black Muslims, he had recanted his teaching that the white man was a devil, he had abandoned his call for a separate black state. I demanded to know just what new gospel he came to proclaim; and just how long could we expect Malcolm to remain convinced of his new found truth. It was a difficult ideological eightball for any debater to surmount.

Malcolm began with *mea culpa.* "I am guilty," he said, "I have allowed myself to be used by Elijah Muhammad." Then he proceeded to ignore me and mount a brilliant attack upon the Johnson administration in particular and the State Department policy as a whole. At the peak of his initial speech Malcolm described America as a "ship full of holes, and a vessel whose captain is insane. Any rational man, any intelligent man," Malcolm continued, "would find some way to get off the ship."

I countered by saying the ship was mine, also, and that I was out to both capture and save the ship.

"Lomax," Malcolm fired back at me, "how are

you going to do something with America the white
man can't do; how can you make the American
dream come true when the architects of that dream
cannot make it come true?"

Malcolm's solution, of course, was that the civil
rights struggle be internationalized. Malcolm and I
had debated publicly some two dozen times since
we first met. The Chicago speech was, by far, the
most eloquent and brilliant performance he ever
mounted.

We left the rear of the hall under heavy police
protection and were spirited to the home of Dr.
T. R. M. Howard; Dr. Howard was my host and had
planned an elaborate party for Malcolm and me.
Some of the best black and white minds gathered at
the Howard's luxurious apartment in Lake Mea-
dows and we had an intellectuals' busman's holiday
that lasted into the early hours of the morning. And
the session ended when it did only because a
physically tired and mentally weary Malcolm
elected to return to his hotel and rest.

I don't recall saying "goodbye" to Malcolm as he
left the apartment. As I recall it he quietly slipped
away while I was locked in verbal combat with a
University of Chicago professor. Saying "goodbye"
was not important to either Malcolm or me. I don't
think it occurred to either of us that we might
never meet again.

Six weeks after the Chicago debate I moved from
New York to Los Angeles. I read with increasing
interest and growing concern about Malcolm's second trip to Africa and his troubles at home. On at
least two occasions I called his wife, Sister Betty, to
express my apprehensions. She, too, was concerned
but she remained firm in the faith that all would be
well once Malcolm returned home. I gave her my

unlisted telephone number in Los Angeles but, as I was to learn all too late, she misplaced it.

On January 28, 1965, I was lecturing at Valley State College, only twenty miles from my home. Little did I know that on that very day a distraught Malcolm X was in a Los Angeles hotel room trying to find me. Only after his death would Edward Bradley, one of the two trusted men who were with Malcolm in the Los Angeles hotel room, relate to me Malcolm's efforts to locate me. I can only conclude, and the record supports this conclusion, that Malcolm was not thinking clearly. My aunt and uncle, James and Laura Hardon, had hosted a party for Malcolm and me when we debated in Los Angeles in 1962. Malcolm could have found me through them. The Reverend Mr. James Hargette, minister of the Church of Christian Fellowship, had become a friend to both Malcolm and me. Malcolm could have found me through Jim Hargette. Ed Bradley and Allen Jamel, the men who were with Malcolm, were unable to locate me but had Malcolm contacted any one of a number of people whom we both knew—even the local chapter of the NAACP—I would have been instantly available.

Sister Betty was to tell me later that Malcolm wanted to "give you some information about something." By then he was dead and I did not ask her what the "something" was.

Thirteen days after he left Los Angeles Malcolm returned to New York from France and England. In the interim Malcolm had visited Chicago, Selma, Paris and London. The date was Saturday, February 13, 1965, the beginning of Big Red's last week on earth.

Shortly after two o'clock that Sunday morning the front end of Malcolm's home exploded with an earth-shaking blast and belched flames. Someone had thrown a fire bomb. Malcolm X leaped from his bed, gathered his terrified family and fled with them through the back door. Firemen battled the flames for more than an hour while Malcolm and his family took refuge in the home of a neighbor. Sister Betty was then pregnant, yet Malcolm left her and his four children in the friend's home and took an early morning plane to Detroit where he was scheduled to speak at a meeting sponsored by the Afro-American Broadcasting Company.

This was Malcolm's last major public appearance before an all black audience and there is a sense in which it encapsuled his life. Only a driven man would have left his family under such circumstances; only a man obsessed with the compulsion to preach a gospel would have appeared before this Detroit audience dressed in a rumpled suit and an open-neck sweater shirt. A man such as Malcolm lectures for one of two reasons—to earn a handsome fee or to spread a gospel. And the Afro-American Broadcasting Company is little more than a tape recorder owned by Detroit attorney Milton Henry. The record is not available but I doubt that Malcolm received much more than his air fare for the Detroit lecture. What gospel, then, was Malcolm X so compulsively driven to spread?

The Detroit speech totally reveals the Malcolm X of the last days; his sight was clear but his thoughts were in disarray. He reflected warmly about Elijah Muhammad and the Black Muslims yet he left no doubt that the movement was enveloped in scandal. Then Malcolm went on to reveal for the first time that he had been actively establishing organizations all over Europe and Africa. Because the speech is a major summation of the man that was Malcolm I have elected to print it in its entirety:

Attorney Milton Henry, distinguished guests, brothers and sister, ladies and gentlemen, friends and enemies: I want to point out first that I am very happy to be here this evening and I am thankful to the Afro-American Broadcasting Company for the invitation to come here this evening. As Attorney Milton Henry has stated—I should say Brother Milton Henry because that's what he is, our brother —I was in a house last night that was bombed, my own. It didn't destroy all my clothes but you know what fire and smoke do to things. The only thing I could get my hands on before leaving was what I have on now.

It isn't something that made me lose confidence in what I am doing, because my wife understands and I have children from this size on down, and even in their young age they understand. I think they would rather have a father or brother or whatever the situation may be who will take a stand in the face of reaction from any narrow-minded people rather than to compromise and later on have to grow up in shame and disgrace.

So I ask you to excuse my appearance. I don't normally come out in front of people without a shirt and tie. I guess that's somewhat a holdover from the Black Muslim movement which I was in. That's one of the good aspects of that movement. It teaches you to be very careful and conscious of how you look, which is a positive contribution on their part. But that positive contribution on their part is greatly offset by too many liabilities.

Also, last night, when the temperature was about 20 above and when this explosion took place, I was caught in what I had on—some pajamas. In trying to get my family out of the house, none of us stopped for any clothes at that point, so we were out in the 20 degree cold. I got them into the house of the neighbor next door. I thought perhaps being in that condition for so long I would get pneumonia or a cold or something like that, so a doctor came today, a nice doctor, and shot something in my arm that naturally put me to sleep. I've been back there asleep ever since the program started in order to get back in shape. So if I have a tendency to stutter or slow down, it's still the effect of that drug. I don't know what kind it was, but it was good; it makes you sleep and there's nothing like sleeping through a whole lot of excitement.

Tonight one of the things that has to be stressed, which has not only the United States very much worried but also has France, Great Britain and most of the powers who formerly were known as colonial powers worried, and that is the African revolution. They are more concerned with the revolution that is taking place in the African continent than they are with the revolution in Asia and in Latin America. And this is because there are so many people of African ancestry within the domestic confines or jurisdictions of these various governments. There is an increasing number of dark-skinned people in England and also in France.

When I was in Africa in May, I noticed a tendency on the part of the Afro-Americans to—what I call lollygag. Everybody else who was over there had something on the ball, something they were doing, something constructive. Let's take Ghana as an example. There would be many refugees in Ghana from South Africa. Some were being trained in how to be soldiers but others were involved as a pressure group or lobby group to let the people of Ghana never forget what happened to the brother in South Africa. Also you had brothers there from Angola and Mozambique. All of the Africans who were exiles from their particular country and would be in a place like Ghana or Tanganyika, now Tanzania—they would be training. Their every move would be designed to offset what was happening to their people back home where they had left. When they escaped from their respective countries that were still colonized, they didn't try and run away from the family; as soon as they got where they were going, they began to organize into pressure groups to get support at the international level against the injustices they were experiencing back home.

But the American Negroes or the Afro-Americans, who were in these various countries, some working for this government, some working for that government, some in business—they were just socializing, they had turned their back on the cause over here, they were partying, you know. When I went through one country in particular, I heard a lot of their complaints and I didn't make any move. But when I got to another country, I found the Afro-Americans there were making the same complaints. So we sat down and talked and we organized a branch in this particular country of the Organization of Afro-American Unity. That one was the only one in existence at that time. Then during the summer when I went back to Africa, I was able in each country that I visited to get the Afro-American community together and organize them and make them aware of their responsibility to those of us who are still here in the lion's den.

They began to do this quite well, and when I got

to Paris and London—there are many Afro-Americans in Paris, and many in London—in November, we organized a group in Paris and within a very short time they had grown into a well-organized unit. In conjunction with the African community, they invited me to Paris Tuesday to address a large gathering of Parisians and Afro-Americans and people from the Caribbean and also from Africa who were interested in our struggle in this country and the rate of progress that we have been making. But the French government and the British government and this government here, the United States, know that I have been almost fanatically stressing the importance of the Afro-Americans uniting with the Africans and working as a coalition, especially in areas which are of mutual benefit to all of us. And the governments in these different places were frightened.

I might point out here that colonialism or imperialism, as the slave system of the West is called, is not something that is just confined to England or France or the United States. The interests in this country are in cahoots with the interests in France and the interests in Britain. It's one huge complex or combine, and it creates what's known not as the American power structure or the French power structure, but an international power structure. This international power structure is used to suppress the masses of dark-skinned people all over the world and exploit them of their natural resources, so that the era in which you and I have been living during the past ten years most specifically has witnessed the upsurge on the part of the black man in Africa against the power structure.

He wants his freedom and now. Mind you, the power structure is international, and its domestic

*base is in London, in Paris, in Washington, D.C.,
and so forth. The outside or external phase of the
revolution which is manifest in the attitude and
action of the Africans today is troublesome enough.
The revolution on the outside of the house, or the
outside of the structure, is troublesome enough. But
now the powers that be are beginning to see that
this struggle on the outside by the black man is
affecting, infecting the black man who is on the
inside of that structure—I hope you understand
what I am trying to say. The newly awakened
people all over the world pose a problem for what
is known as Western interests, which is imperialism,
colonialism, racism and all these other negative
isms or vulturistic isms. Just as the external forces
pose a grave threat, they can now see that the
internal forces pose an even greater threat. But the
internal forces pose an even greater threat only
when they have properly analyzed the situation and
know what the stakes really are.*

*Just advocating a coalition of African, Afro-
Americans, Arabs, and Asians who live within the
structure automatically has upset France, which is
supposed to be one of the most liberal countries on
earth, and it made them expose their hand. England is the same way. And I don't have to tell you
about this country that we are living in now. When
you count the number of dark-skinned people in
the Western hemisphere you can see that there are
probably over 100 million. When you consider Bra-
zil has two-thirds what we call colored, or non-
white, and Venezuela, Honduras and other Central
American countries, Cuba and Jamaica, and the
United States and even Canada—when you total all
these people up, you have probably over 100 million. And this 100 million on the inside of the power*

structure today is what is causing a great deal of
concern for the power structure itself.

We thought that the first thing to do was to unite
our people, not only internally, but with our brothers
and sisters abroad. It was for that purpose that I
spent five months in the Middle East and Africa
during the summer. The trip was very enlightening,
inspiring, and fruitful. I didn't go into any African
country, or any country in the Middle East for that
matter, and run into any closed door, closed mind,
or closed heart. I found a warm reception and an
amazingly deep interest and sympathy for the black
man in this country in regards to our struggle for
human rights.

I hope you will forgive me for speaking so infor-
mally tonight, but I frankly think it is always better
to be informal. As far as I am concerned, I can
speak to people better in an informal way than I
can with all of this stiff formality that ends up meaning nothing. Plus, when people are informal, they
are relaxed. When they are relaxed, their mind is
more open, and they can weigh things more objec-
tively. Whenever you and I are discussing our problems we need to be very objective, very cool, calm
and collected. That doesn't mean we should always
be. There is a time to be cool and a time to be hot.
See—you get messed up into thinking that there is
only one time for everything. There is a time to love
and a time to hate. Even Solomon said that, and
he was in that book, too. You're just taking something
out of the book that fits your cowardly nature when
you don't want to fight, and you say, "Well, Jesus
said don't fight." But I don't even believe Jesus said
that.

Before I get involved in anything nowadays, I have
to straighten out my own position, which is

clear. I am not a racist in any form whatsoever. I don't believe in any form of racism. I don't believe in any form of discrimination or segregation. I believe in Islam. I am a Muslim and there is nothing wrong with being a Muslim, nothing wrong with the religion of Islam. It just teaches us to believe in Allah as the God. Those of you who are Christians probably believe in the same God, because I think you believe in the God who created the universe. That's the one we believe in, the one who created the universe—the only difference being you call him God and we call him Allah. The Jews call him Jehovah. If you could understand Hebrew, you would probably call him Jehovah, too. If you could understand Arabic, you would probably call him Allah. But since the white man, your friend, took your language away from you during slavery, the only language you know is his language. You know your friend's language, so when he's putting the rope around your neck, you call for God and he calls for God. And you wonder why the one you call on never answers.

Elijah Muhammad had taught us that the white man could not enter into Mecca in Arabia and all of us who followed him, we believed it. When I got over there and went to Mecca and saw these people who were blond and blue-eyed and pale-skinned and all those things, I said, "Well," but I watched them closely. And I noticed that though they were white, and they would call themselves white, there was a difference between them and the white ones over here. And that basic difference was this: In Asia or the Arab world or in Africa, where the Muslims are, if you find one who says he's white, all he's doing is using an adjective to describe something that's incidental about him, one of his inci-

*dental characteristics; there is nothing else to it,
he's just white.*

*But when you get the white man over here in
America and he says he's white, he means something else. You can listen to the sound of his voice
—when he says he's white, he means he's boss.
That's right. That's what white means in this language. You know the expression, "free, white and
twenty-one." He made that up. He's letting you
know that white means free, boss. He's up there, so
that when he says he's white he has a little different
sound in his voice. I know you know what I'm
talking about.*

*Despite the fact that I saw that Islam was a
religion of brotherhood, I also had to face reality.
And when I got back into this American society,
I'm in a society that might preach it on Sunday, but
they don't practice it on any day. America is a
society where there is no brotherhood. This society
is controled primarily by the racists and segregationists who are in Washington, D.C.; they exercise
the same forms of brutal oppression against dark-
skinned people in South and North Vietnam, or in
the Congo, or in Cuba or any other place on this
earth where they are trying to exploit and oppress.
That is a society whose government doesn't hesitate
to inflict the most brutal form of punishment and
oppression upon dark-skinned people all over the
world.*

*Look right now what's going on in and around
Saigon and Hanoi and in the Congo and elsewhere.
They are violent when their interests are at stake.
But all that violence they display at the international level; when you and I want just a little bit of
freedom, we're supposed to be nonviolent. They're
violent in Korea, they're violent in Germany, they're*

violent in the South Pacific, they're violent in Cuba, they're violent wherever they go. But when it comes time for you and me to protect ourselves against lynchings, they tell us to be nonviolent.

That's a shame. Because we get tricked into being nonviolent, and when somebody stands up and talks like I just did, they say, "Why, he's advocating violence." Isn't that what they say? Everytime you pick up your newspaper, you see where one of these things has written into it that I am advocating violence. I have never advocated any violence. I have only said that black people who are the victims of organized violence perpetrated upon us by the Klan, the Citizens Councils, and many other forms, should defend ourselves. And when I say we should defend ourselves against the violence of others, they use their press skillfully to make the world think that I am calling for violence, period. I wouldn't call on anybody to be violent without a cause. But I think all black men in this country, above and beyond people all over the world, will be more justified when he stands up and starts to protect himself, no matter how many necks he has to break and heads he has to crack.

The Klan is a cowardly outfit. They have perfected the art of making Negroes be afraid, the Klan is safe. But the Klan itself is cowardly. One of them never comes after one of you. They all come together. They're scared of you. And you sit there when they're putting the rope around your neck saying, "Forgive them, Lord, they know not what they do." As long as they've been doing it, they're experts at it, they know what they're doing. No, since the federal government has shown that it isn't going to do anything about it but talk, then it is a duty, it's your and my duty as men, as human beings, it is our duty to our people, to organize ourselves and let the government know that if they don't stop that Klan, we'll stop it ourselves. Then you'll see the government start doing something about it. But don't ever think that they're going to do it just on some kind of morality basis. No. So I don't believe in violence—that's why I want to stop it. And can't stop it with love, not love of those things down there. No! So, we only mean vigorous action in self-defense, and that vigorous action we feel we're justified in initiating by any means necessary.

Now, for saying something like that, the press calls us racist and people who are "violent in reverse." This is how they psycho you. They make you think that if you try to stop the Klan from lynching you, you're practicing violence in reverse. Pick up on this, I hear a lot of you parrot what the man says. You say, "I don't want to be a Ku Klux Klan in reverse." Well, if a criminal comes around your house with his gun, brother, just because he's got a gun and he's robbing your house, and he's a robber, it doesn't make you a robber because you grab your gun and run him out. No, the man is using some tricky logic on you. I say it is time for black people to put together the type of action, the unity, that is necessary to pull the sheet off of them so they won't be frightening black people any longer. That's all. And when we say this, the press calls us "racist in reverse. Don't struggle except within the ground rules that the people you're struggling against have laid down." Why, this is insane, but it shows how they can do it. With skillful manipulating of the press they're able to make the victim look like the criminal and the criminal look like the victim.

Right now in New York we have a couple of cases where the police grabbed a brother and beat him unmercifully—and charged him with assaulting them. They used the press to make it look like he is the criminal and they are the victims. This is how they do it, and if you study how they do it here, then you'll know how they do it over there. It's the same game going all the time, and if you and I don't awaken and see what this man is doing to us, then it will be too late. They may have the gas ovens built before you realize that they're already hot.

One of the shrewd ways that they project us in the image of a criminal is that they take statistics and with the press feed these statistics to the public, primarily the white public. Because there are some well-meaning persons in the white public as well as bad-meaning persons in the white public. And whatever the government is going to do, it always wants the public on its side—whether it is the local government, state government or federal government. At the local level, they will create an image by feeding statistics to the public through the press showing the high crime rate in the Negro community. As soon as this high crime rate is emphasized through the press, then people begin to look upon the Negro community as a community of criminals.

And then any Negro in the community can be stopped in the street. "Put your hands up," and they pat you down. Might be a doctor, a lawyer, a preacher or some other kind of Uncle Tom, but despite your professional standing, you'll find that you're the same victim as the man who's in the alley. Just because you're black and you live in a black community which has been projected as a community of criminals. And once the public accepts this image, it also paves the way for police-state type of activity in the Negro community—they can use any kind of brutal methods to suppress blacks because they're criminals anyway. And what has given us this image? The press again, by letting the power structure or the racist element in the power structure use them in their way.

A very good example was the riots that took place during the summer. I was in Africa, I read about them over there. If you noticed, they referred to the rioters as vandals, hoodlums, thieves, and they skillfully took the burden off the society for its failure to correct these negative conditions in the black community. They took the burden completely off the society and put it right on the community by using the press to make it appear that the looting and all of this was proof that the whole act was nothing but vandals and robbers and thieves, who weren't really interested in anything other than that which was negative. And I hear many dumb, brain-washed Negroes who parrot the same old party line that the man handed down in his paper.

It was not the case that they were just knocking out store windows ignorantly. In Harlem, for instance, all of the stores are owned by white people. The black people are just there—paying rent, buying the groceries; but they don't own the stores, clothing stores, food stores, any kind of stores; don't even own the homes that they live in. These are all owned by outsiders, and for these run-down apartment dwellings, the black man in Harlem pays more money than the man down in the rich Park Avenue section. It costs us more money to live in the slums than it costs them to live down on Park Avenue. Black people in Harlem know this, and *that the white merchants charge us more money for food in Harlem—and it's the cheap food, the worst food; we have to pay more money for it than the man has to pay for it downtown. So black people know that they're being expoited and that their blood is being sucked and they see no way out.*

When the thing is finally sparked, the white man is not there—he's gone. The merchant is not there, the landlord is not there, the one they consider to be the enemy isn't there. So, they knock at his property. This is what makes them knock down the store windows and set fire to things, and things of that sort. It's not that they're thieves. But they (the newspapers) are trying to project the image to the public that this is being done by thieves, and thieves alone. It's a corrupt, vicious, hypocritical system that has castrated the black man, and the only way the black man can get back at it is to strike it in the only way he knows how.

(When I say) they use the press, that doesn't mean that all reporters are bad. Some of them are good, I suppose. But you can take their collective approach to any problem and see that they can always agree when it gets to you and me. They knew that the Afro-American Broadcasting Company was giving this affair—which is designed to honor outstanding black Americans, is it not? But you find nothing in the newspapers that gives the slightest hint, though there are supposed to be many sources of news. If you don't think that they're in cahoots, watch. They're all interested, or none of them are interested. It's not a staggering thing. They're not going to say anything in advance about an affair that's being given by any black people who believe in functioning beyond the scope of the

*ground rules that are laid down by the liberal
elements of the power structure.*

*When you start thinking for yourselves you
frighten them, and they try and block your getting
to the public, for the fear that if the public listens
to you then the public won't listen to them anymore. And they've got certain Negroes whom they
have to keep blowing up in the papers to make
them look like leaders. So that the people will keep
on following them, no matter how many knocks
they get on their heads following them. This is how
the man does it, and if you don't wake up and find
out how he does it, I tell you, they'll be building
gas chambers and gas ovens pretty soon—I don't
mean those kind you've got at home in your kitchen
—(and) you'll be in one of them, just like the Jews
ended up in gas ovens over there in Germany.
You're in a society that's just as capable of building
gas ovens for black people as Hitler's society was.*

*Now what effect does (the struggle over Africa)
have on us? Why should the black man in America
concern himself since he's been away from the
African continent for three or four hundred years?
Why should we concern ourselves? What impact
does what happens to them have upon us? Number
one, you have to realize that up until 1959 Africa
was dominated by the colonial powers. Having
complete control over Africa, the colonial powers of
Europe projected the image of Africa negatively.
They always project Africa in a negative light:
jungle savages, cannibals, nothing civilized. Why
then naturally it was so negative that it was negative to you and me, and you and I began to hate it.
We didn't want anybody telling us anything about
Africa, much less calling us Africans. In hating
Africa and in hating the Africans, we ended up*

can't have a positive attitude toward yourself and a negative attitude toward Africa at the same time. To the same degree that your understanding of and attitude toward Africa become positive, you'll find that your understanding of and your attitude to- hating ourselves, without even realizing it. Because you can't hate the roots of a tree, and not hate the tree. You can't hate your origin and not end up hating yourself. You can't hate Africa and not hate yourself.

You show me one of these people over here who has been thoroughly brainwashed and has a nega- tive attitude toward Africa, and I'll show you one who has a negative attitude toward himself. You ward yourself will also become positive. And this is what the white man knows. So they very skillfully make you and me hate our African identity, our African characteristics.

You know yourself that we have been a people who hated our African characteristics. We hated our heads, we hated the shape of our nose, we wanted one of those long dog-like noses, you know; we hated the color of our skin, hated the blood of Africa that was in our veins. And in hating our features and our skin and our blood, why, we had to end up hating ourselves. And we hated our- selves. Our color became to us a chain—we felt that it was holding us back; our color became to us like a prison which we felt was keeping us confined, not letting us go this way or that way. We felt that all of these restrictions were based solely upon our color, and the psychological reaction to that would have to be that as long as we felt imprisoned or chained or trapped by black skin, black features and black blood, that skin and those features and that blood holding us back atuomatically had to become hateful to us. And it became hateful to us.

It made us feel inferior; it made us feel inadequate; made us feel helpless. And when we fell victims to this feeling of inadequacy or inferiority or helplessness, we turned to somebody else to show us the way. We didn't have confidence in another black man to show us the way, or black people to show us the way. In those days we didn't. We didn't think a black man could do anything except play some horns—you know, make some sound and make you happy with some songs, and in that way. But in serious things, where our food, clothing, shelter and education were concerned, we turned to the man. We never thought in terms of bringing these things into existence for ourselves, we never thought in terms of doing things for ourselves. Because we felt helpless. What made us feel helpless was our hatred for ourselves. And our hatred for ourselves stemmed from our hatred for things African.

After 1959 the spirit of African nationalism was fanned to a high flame and we then began to witness the complete collapse of colonialism. France began to get out of French West Africa, Belgium began to make moves to get out of the Congo, Britian began to make moves to get out of Kenya, Tanganyika, Uganda, Nigeria and some of these other places. And although it looked like they were getting out, they pulled a trick that was colossal.

When you're playing ball and they've got you trapped, you don't throw the ball away—you throw it to one of your teammates who's in the clear. And this is what the European powers did. They were trapped on the African continent, they couldn't stay there—they were looked upon as colonial and im-

perialist. They had to pass the ball to someone whose image was different, and they passed the ball to Uncle Sam. And he picked it up and has been running it for a touchdown ever since. He was in the clear, he was not looked upon as one who had colonized the African continent. At that time, the Africans couldn't see that though the United States hadn't colonized the African continent, it had colonized 22 million blacks here on this continent. Because we're just as thoroughly colonized as anybody else.

When the ball was passed to the United States, it was passed at the time when John Kennedy came into power. He picked it up and helped to run it. He was one of the shrewdest backfield runners that history has ever recorded. He surrounded himself with intellectuals—highly educated, learned and well-informed people. And their analysis told him that the government of America was confronted with a new problem. And this new problem stemmed from the fact the Africans were now awakened, they were enlightened, they were fearless, they would fight. This meant that the Western powers couldn't stay there by force. Since their own economy, the European economy and the American economy, was based upon their continued influence over the African continent, they had to find some means of staying there. So they used the friendly approach.

They switched from the old openly colonial imperialistic approach to the benevolent approach. They came up with some benevolent colonialism, philanthropic colonialism, humanitarianism, or dollarism. Immediately everything was Peace Corps, Operation Crossroads, "We've got to help our African brothers." Pick up on that: Can't help us in

Mississippi. Can't help us in Alabama, or Detroit, or out here in Dearborn where some real Ku Klux Klan lives. They're going to send all the way to Africa to help. I know Dearborn; you know, I'm from Detroit. I used to live out here in Inkster. And you had to go through Dearborn to get to Inkster. Just like driving through Mississippi when you got to Dearborn. Is it still that way? Well, you should straighten it out.

So, realizing that it was necessary to come up with these new approaches, Kennedy did it. He created an image of himself that was skillfully designed to make the people on the African continent think he was Jesus, the great white father, come to make things right. I'm telling you, some of these Negroes cried harder when he died than they cried for Jesus when he was crucified. From 1954 to 1964 was the era in which we witnessed the merging of Africa. The impact that this had on the civil-rights struggle in America has never been fully told.

For one thing, one of the primary ingredients in the complete civil-rights struggle was the Black Muslim movement. The Black Muslim movement took no part in things political, civic—it didn't take too much part in anything other than stopping people from doing this drinking, smoking, and so on. Moral reform it had, but beyond that it did nothing. But it talked such a strong talk that it put the other Negro organizations on the spot. Before the Black Muslim movement came along, the NAACP was looked upon as radical; they were getting ready to investigate it. And then along came the Muslim movement and frightened the white man so hard that he began to say, "Thank God for old Uncle Roy, and Uncle Whitney and Uncle A. Philip and Uncle"—you've got a whole lot of uncles *in there; I can't remember their names, they're all older than I so I call them "uncle." Plus, if you use the word "Uncle Tom" nowadays, I hear they can sue you for libel, you know. So I don't call any of them Uncle Tom anymore. I call them Uncle Roy.*

One of the things that made the Black Muslim movement grow was its emphasis upon things African. This was the secret to the growth of the Black Muslim movement. African blood, African origin, African culture, African ties. And you'd be surprised—we discovered that deep within the subconscious of the black man in this country, he is still more African than he is American. He thinks that he's more American than African, because the man is jiving him, the man is brainwashing him every day. He's telling him, "You're an American, you're an American." Man, how could you think you're an American when you haven't ever had any kind of an American treat over here? You have never, never. Ten men can be sitting at a table eating, you know, dining, and I can come and sit down where they're dining. They're dining; I've got a plate in front of me, but nothing is on it. Because all of us are sitting at the same table, are all of us diners? I'm not a diner until you let me dine. Just being at the table with others who are dining doesn't make me a diner, and this is what you've got to get in your head here in this country.

Just because you're in this country doesn't make you an American. No, you've got to go farther than that before you can become an American. You've got to enjoy the fruits of Americanism, You haven't enjoyed those fruits. You've enjoyed the thorns. You've enjoyed those thistles. But you have not enjoyed the fruits, no sir. You have fought harder for the fruits than the white man has, you have

*worked harder for the fruits than the white man
has, but you've enjoyed less. When the man put the
uniform on you and sent you abroad, you fought
harder than they did. Yes, I know you—when
you're fighting for them you can fight.*

The Black Muslim movement did make that contribution. They made the whole civil-rights movement become more militant and more acceptable to
the white power structure. He would rather have
them than us. In fact, I think we forced many of the
civil-rights leaders to be even more militant than
they intended. I know some of them who get out
there and "boom, boom, boom," and don't mean it.
Because they're right on back in their corner as
soon as the action comes.

John F. Kennedy also saw that it was necessary
for a new approach among the American Negroes.
And during his entire term in office, he specialized
in how to psycho the American Negro. Now, a lot
of you all don't like my saying that—but I wouldn't
ever take a stand on that if I didn't know what I
was talking about. By living in this kind of society,
pretty much around them—and you know what I
mean when I say "them"—I learned to study them.
You can think that they mean you some good
ofttimes, but if you look at it a little closer you'll see
that they don't mean you any good. That doesn't
mean there aren't some of them who mean good.
But it does mean that most of them don't mean
good.

Kennedy's new approach was pretending to go
along with us in our struggle for civil rights. He
was another proponent of rights. But I remember
the exposé that Look magazine did on the Meredith
situation in Mississippi. Look magazine did an exposé showing that Robert Kennedy and Governor

Barnett had made a deal, wherein the Attorney
General was going to come down and try to force
Meredith into school, and Barnett was going to
stand at the door, you know, and say, "No, you
can't come in." He was going to get in anyway, but
it was all arranged in advance and then Barnett
was supposed to keep the support of the white
racists, because that's who he was upholding, and
Kennedy would keep the support of the Negroes,
because that's who he'd be upholding. It was a
cut-and-dried deal. And it's not a secret; it was
written, they write about it. But if that's a deal,
how many other deals do you think go down? What
you think is on the level is crookeder, brothers and
sisters, than a pretzel, which is most crooked.

So in my conclusion I would like to point out that
the approach used by the administration right up
until today was designed skillfully to make it appear they were trying to solve the problem when
they actually weren't. They would deal with the
conditions, but never the cause. They only gave us
tokenism. Tokenism benefits only a few. It never
benefits the masses, and the masses are the ones
who have the problem, not the few. That one who
benefits from tokenism, he doesn't want to be
around us anyway—that's why he picks up on the
token.

The masses of our people still have bad housing,
bad schooling and inferior jobs, jobs that don't
compensate with sufficient salaries for them to carry
on their life in this world. So that the problem for
the masses has gone absolutely unsolved. The only
ones for whom it has been solved are people like
Whitney Young, who is supposed to be placed in
the cabinet, so the rumor says. He'll be the first
black cabinet man. And that answers where he's at.

*And others have been given jobs, like Carl Rowan,
who was put over the USIA, and is very skillfully
trying to make Africans think that the problem of
black men in this country is all solved.*

*The worst thing the white man can do to himself
is to take one of these kinds of Negroes and ask
him, "How do your people feel, boy?" He's going to
tell that man that we are satisfied. That's what they
do, brothers and sisters. They get behind the door
and tell the white man we're satisfied. "Just keep on
keeping me up here in front of them, boss, and I'll
keep them behind you." That's what they talk like
when they're behind closed doors. Because, you
see, the white man doesn't go along with anybody
who's not for him. He doesn't care are you for right
or wrong, he wants to know are you for him. And if
you're for him, he doesn't care what else you're for.
As long as you're for him, then he puts you up over
the Negro community. You become a spokesman.*

*In your struggle it's like standing on a revolving
wheel; you're running, but you're not going anywhere. You run faster and faster and the wheel just
goes faster and faster. You don't ever leave the spot
that you're standing in. So, it is very important for
you and me to see that our problem has to have a
solution that will benefit the masses, not the upper
class—so called upper class. Actually, there's no
such thing as an upper-class Negro. All of them
catch the same hell as the other-class Negro. All of
them catch the same hell, which is one of things
that's good about this racist system—it makes us all
one.*

*If you'd tell them right now what is in store for
1965, they'd think you crazy for sure. But 1965 will
be the longest and hottest and bloodiest year of
them all. It has to be, not because you want it to be,*

or I want it to be, or we want it to be, but because
the conditions that created the explosions in 1963
are still here; the conditions that created explosions
in 1964 are still here. You can't say that you're not
going to have an explosion when you leave the
conditions, the ingredients, still here. As long as
those explosive ingredients remain, then you're going to have the potential for explosion on your
hands.

And, brothers and sisters, let me tell you, I spend
my time out there in the streets with people, all
kinds of people, listening to what they have to say.
And they're getting to the point of frustration
where they begin to feel, "what do we have to
lose?" When you get to that point, you're the type
of person who can create a very dangerously explosive atmosphere. This is what's happening in our
neighborhoods, to our people.

I read in a poll taken by Newsweek magazine
this week, saying that Negroes are satisfied. Oh,
yes, Newsweek, you know, supposed to be a top
magazine with a top pollster, talking about how
satisfied Negroes are. Maybe I haven't met the
Negroes he met. Because I know he hasn't met the
ones that I've met. And this is dangerous. This is
where the white man does himself the most harm.
He invents statistics to create an image, thinking
that that image is going to hold things in check.
You know why they always say Negroes are lazy?
Because they want Negroes to be lazy. And once
they put this thing in the Negro's mind, they feel
that he tries to fulfill their image. If they say you
can't unite black people, and then you come to
them to unite them, they won't unite because it's
been said that they're not supposed to unite. It's a

*psycho that they work, and it's the same way with
these statistics.*

When they think that an explosive era is coming
up, then they grab their press again and begin to
shower the Negro public, to make it appear that all
Negroes are satisfied. Because if you know you're
dissatisfied all by yourself and ten others aren't, you
play it cool; but if you know that all ten of you are
dissatisfied, you get with it. This is what the man
knows. The man knows that if these Negroes find
out how dissatisfied they really are—even Uncle
Tom is dissatisfied, he's just playing his part for
now—this is what makes the man frightened. It
frightens them in France and frightens them in
England, and it frightens them in the United States.

And it is for this reason that it is so important for
you and me to start organizing among ourselves,
intelligently, and try to find out: "What are we
going to do if this happens, that happens or the
next thing happens?" Don't think that you're going
to run to the man and say, "Look, boss, this is me."
Why, when the deal goes down, you'll look just like
me in his eyesight; I'll make it tough for you. Yes,
when the deal goes down, he doesn't look for you.
Yes, when the deal goes down, he doesn't look at
you in any better light than he looks at me.

I point these things out, brothers and sisters, so
that you and I will know the importance in 1965 of
being in complete unity with each other, in harmony with each other, and not letting the man
maneuver us into fighting one another. The situation I have been maneuvered into right now, between me and the Black Muslim movement, is something that I really deeply regret, because I don't
think anything is more destructive than two groups
of black people fighting each other. But it's some-

thing that can't be avoided because it goes deep down beneath the surface, and these things will come up in the very near future.

I might say this before I sit down. If you recall, when I left the Black Muslim movement, I stated clearly that it wasn't my intention to even continue to be aware that they existed; I was going to spend my time working in the non-Muslim community. But they were fearful if they didn't do something that perhaps many of those who were in the (Black Muslim) mosque would leave it and follow a different direction. So they had to start doing a takeoff on me, plus, they had to try and silence me because of what they know that I know. I think that they should know me well enough to know that they certainly can't frighten me. But when it does come to the light—there are some things involving the Black Muslim movement which, when they come to light, will shock you.

The thing that you have to understand about those of us in the Black Muslim movement was that all of us believed 100 percent in the divinity of Elijah Muhammad. We believed in him. We actually believed that God, in Detroit by the way, that God had taught him and all of that. I always believed that he believed it himself. And I was shocked when I found out that he, himself, didn't believe it. And when that shock reached me, then I began to look everywhere else and try and get a better understanding of the things that confront all of us so that we can get together in some kind of way to offset them.

I want to thank you for coming out this evening. I think it's wonderful that as many of you came out, considering the blackout on the meeting that took place. Milton Henry and the brothers who are here

*in Detroit are very progressive young men, and I
would advise all of you to get with them in any
way that you can to try and create some kind of
united effort toward common goals, common objectives. Don't let the power structure maneuver you
into a time-wasting battle with others when you
could be involved in something that is constructive
and getting a real job done.*

*I say again that I'm not a racist, I don't believe in
any form of segregation or anything like that. I'm
for brotherhood for everybody, but I don't believe
in forcing brotherhood upon people who don't want
it. Let us practice brotherhood among ourselves,
and then if others want to practice brotherhood
with us, we're for practicing it with them also. But I
don't think that we should run around trying to
love somebody who doesn't love us.*

Thank you.

How is one to assess Malcolm's lonely thoughts
that Sunday night as he took a late flight back to
New York? If he were not mentally disturbed before the bombing the events of the last twenty-four
hours were sufficient to make even the gods of
Olympus into madmen. Yet Malcolm spent Monday
methodically rehousing his family and preparing
for a speech he was to deliver before the meeting of
his Organization of Afro-American Unity at the
Audubon Ballroom. As Alex Haley, Malcolm's biographer, observed, the man who spoke at the Audubon on Monday night, February 15, was not the
poised and imperturbable platform artist both Haley and I had known for years: For in addition to
all else, Malcolm returned to New York from Detroit only to discover that Minister James X, the
man who had replaced him as Minister of Temple

Number Seven in Harlem, had told the press that Malcolm had fire-bombed his own home "to get publicity."

"I have reached the end of my rope!" Malcolm told the audience of several hundred persons. "I wouldn't care for myself if they would not harm my family." Then as the audience sat in shocked silence Malcolm shouted, "My home was bombed by the Muslims!" And Big Red went on to declare war. "Just as there are hunters, there are those who hunt the hunters!"

Harlem was on the brink of a major crisis, for every evidence indicated the imminent outbreak of gang warfare between the Black Muslims and the followers of Malcolm X. The two groups had been on the verge of open clashes for more than a month, since Malcolm's telephone had been mysteriously cut off. At that time followers of Malcolm forced a confrontation with Black Muslims in front of the Muslims' restaurant on Lennox Avenue. The police arrived in time to prevent open violence but guns were found in the car driven by Malcolm's followers and six of them were arrested.

But the fire bombing of Malcolm's home was a far more serious matter. Both the police and the Black Muslims themselves placed guards around the restaurant as well as the Mosque, located just around the corner on 116th Street.

On Tuesday Malcolm called Alex Haley who was then living in upstate New York and said: "I have been marked for death within the next five days. I have the names of five Muslims who have been chosen to kill me. I will announce them at the meeting next Sunday."

Later that same day Malcolm told yet another friend: "I'm going to apply to the police for a

permit to carry a pistol. I don't know if they'll let
me have one or not, as I served time in prison."

Malcolm spent most of Wednesday in his shabby
OAAU office trying to untangle his organizational
problems. His protracted absences, his troubled
private life, and—yes—his inability as an organizer
had rendered the group impotent. And as Malcolm
worked there was near him an office bulletin board
which read: "Bro. Malcolm Speaks Thurs. Feb. 18,
WINS Station, 10:30 P.M."

Thursday morning Malcolm visited a real estate
agent to discuss buying a home. His chilling experiences since leaving Elijah had not only changed
Malcolm's public philosophy; it had altered his
attitude toward his family as well. In a moving
moment Malcolm confessed to Alex Haley that he
had not been a good father and husband, that he
had been away from home too much, that he had
been *too busy*. Malcolm felt an obligation to buy
Sister and the children a home. He had no money
yet he made a date with the real estate broker to go
house shopping on Saturday.

Midafternoon on Thursday Malcolm gave yet
another interview. "I am man enough to tell you,"
Malcolm said to the reporter, "that I can't put my
finger on exactly what my philosophy is now, but I
am flexible."

Thursday night Malcolm subjected himself to the
mental and psychological brutalities that are inher-
ent in most radio "talk" programs. What his OAAU
had extravagantly billed as "Bro. Malcolm Speaks"
was actually a telephone-call-in radio show on
which Malcolm and two other men appeared as
guests. The other participants were Aubrey Bar-
nette, an ex-Black Muslim who had just written an
article, "The Black Muslims Are A Fraud," for the

Saturday Evening Post, and Gordon Hall, a self-styled "expert on extremist organizations."

The first sharp exchange came when Stan Bernard, the host of the radio program, asked Gordon Hall to evaluate the Black Muslim organization:

HALL: Well, to be perfectly frank with you, and I do believe in speaking frankly, I think at the moment the Muslims are a dying organization, they're on the way out, they've made no impact in the Negro community nationally at any point, and even less so now. Malcolm had no place to go, which is why he's floundering so badly. For example, he's been breaking bread with the communists downtown—

MALCOLM: What communists, what communists have I been—

HALL: Socialist Workers Party—

MALCOLM: You are absolutely out of your mind, I have never broken bread with—

HALL: You have given several speeches which they have reprinted—

MALCOLM: Well, that's not breaking bread. I speak anywhere, I spoke in London, England, and—

HALL: You were very glad to go back several times, and they are reprinting one of your major addresses in *The Militant*—

MALCOLM: I spoke in a church, I spoke in a church in Rochester a couple of nights ago. Does that make me a Methodist?—

HALL: We're not talking about churches, we're talking about the Socialist Workers Party—

MALCOLM: Just because you speak somewhere doesn't make you that. You speak to the public and you speak on any platform—

HALL: Oh, I don't, Malcolm.

MALCOLM:—and I speak to the public and I
speak on any platform.
HALL: I'm afraid that's not the case, Malcolm.
MALCOLM: If speaking on the socialist platform
makes me a socialist, then when I speak in a
Methodist church—
HALL: It was a communist platform—
MALCOLM: I was in Selma, Alabama, last week,
speaking in Martin Luther King's church. Does that
make me a follower of Martin Luther King? No,
your line of reasoning, sir, doesn't fit me.

That was the afternoon hundreds of black students rioted in Brooklyn because of "segregated
school conditions."

But what "line of reasoning" did fit Malcolm?
Hall fully recognized Malcolm's philosophical indi-
cisiveness and unleashed a scathing verbal attack:

HALL: Well, at any rate, they're floundering now,
and there's a lot of internecine warfare going on in
the Harlem section, and most of the movements are
small and splintered, and are splinters of splinters.
And I suppose only the future will tell which one
will emerge victorious and perhaps claim the most
members. I would make a prediction, and I think
we could come back a year from now, Stan, and I
think you may find Malcolm preaching a completely separate doctrine and leading some other kind of
movement.
MALCOLM: Well, you know, one of the best com-
pliments that Dr. Hall here can pay me is just the
things that he says. When he begins to pat me on
the back, I'll be worried—
HALL: I'm not patting you on the back. I told you
up in Boston—

MALCOLM: —I said, when you begin to pat me on the back—

HALL: —give a little time and you'd be preaching a new line, and you are.

MALCOLM: I said, when you begin to pat me on the back, I'll be worried. When you begin, people of your profession, who make a profession out of dealing with groups in this country. When you begin to pat me on the back, then I'll be worried, sir. Now I would advise you, if you think that nationalism has no influence whatsoever, the nationalists, the Organization of Afro-American Unity, are having a rally at the Audubon Ballroom on Broadway—

HALL: I think you mentioned it earlier, you're getting in a couple of plugs.

MALCOLM: I'm going to mention it again. I wouldn't come on the program and not mention it. Because one of the most difficult things for nationalists to do is to let the public know what they're doing. So we're having this rally at the Audubon—

HALL: The public is engaged in a vast conspiracy against you; it's obvious from what you say—

MALCOLM: You're going to make me mention it four or five times. We're having this rally at the Audubon Ballroom this coming Sunday at two o'clock and people just like you, who consider themselves experts on nationalists, are given front-seat invitations, and I would advise you, since it's your profession to know what nationalists and other so-called extremists are doing, to come and be our guest. Now, one thing I'd like to point out to you, Dr. Hall whenever you find black—

HALL: You know perfectly well I'm not a doctor, Malcolm.

MALCOLM: Well, you sound like you're an expert

on something, I thought you were a doctor. Whenever you find the condition that black people are confronted by in this country, being permitted by the government to exist so long, the condition in itself is extreme—and any black man, who really feels about this situation that our people are confronted by, his feelings are extreme. You can't take a cough syrup and cure somebody who has pneumonia. And the black people are becoming more extreme every day. I was in Alabama a couple of weeks ago, before I went to England, down there with Dr. King and some of the others, who are trying to just register and vote. Now I'll tell you frankly, with King supposed to be the most moderate, most conservative, most loving, most endorsed, supported—

HALL: The word is responsible, but go ahead.

MALCOLM: O.K., responsible to the white power structure. To me, when white people talk about responsible—

HALL: He's a responsible American, that's what he is.

MALCOLM: When people like you usually refer to Negroes as responsible, you mean Negroes who are responsible in the context of your type of thinking. So, getting right back to Dr. King, any time you find a person who goes along with the government to the degree that Dr. King does, and still Dr. King's followers, children, are made to run down the road by brute policemen who are nothing but Klansmen, and the federal government can step in and do nothing about it, I will guarantee you that you are producing extremists by the thousands. Now when I was down there, they wanted me to speak to the press, but didn't want me to speak to the church, or the children or the students. It was the students themselves that insisted that I speak, that gave me the opportuntiy to speak.

That, of course, was not the operation of the first-class Malcolm mind that had debated me for five years. On a better day Malcolm would have torn Hall to shreds. But by then Malcolm was so unsure of himself and his beliefs that he became a punching bag for a white man who made a profession out of knowing what extremist black men were doing. Instead of counter punching—and Malcolm had all the amunition on his side—Malcolm rejoindered with banal and inconsequential thrusts over whether Hall was a "doctor." And it was not a strong and confident Malcolm who went to such repetitious lengths to advertise his forthcoming rally at the Audubon Ballroom.

During the next exchange it became abundantly clear why militant black youths refused to ally with Malcolm. Malcolm had charged that American society was creating young black extremists by the thousands. Then Stan Bernard interjected a question:

BERNARD: How? You mean—I know you're talking about these children being made into extremists —but how, how is the situation going to be changed? Do you think by warfare?

MALCOLM: It's not going to be changed by making believe that it doesn't exist to the intense degree that it exists. And it's not going to be changed by putting out polls, like *Newsweek* magazine did last week, implying that Negroes are satisfied with the rate of progress. This is deluding yourself. And my contention is that white people do themselves a disservice by putting out these kinds of things to make it appear that Negroes are satisfied when the most explosive situation, racially, that has ever existed in this country, exists right now. And all of your so-called responsible leaders, when they speak about the situation, they say everything is in check. Yet every day you find Negro children becoming more explosive than ever—

BERNARD: You're not answering my question, you're avoiding it. I asked you how is it going to change? Is it going to change through extreme behavior, let's call it extreme reaction—in other words, you are going to react extremely to a situation that you don't like? Now, how extreme can your reaction be?

MALCOLM: Well, sir, when Russia put missiles in Cuba, the only thing that made Russia get her missiles out of Cuba was when America pointed missiles right back at Russia.

BERNARD: Are you suggesting revolution?

MALCOLM: No, I'm saying this: That when you respect the intelligence of black people in this country as being equal to that of whites, then you will realize that the reaction of the black man to oppression will be the same as the reaction of the white man to oppression. The white man will not turn the other cheek when he's being oppressed. He will not practice any kind of love of a Klan or a Citizens Council or anyone else. But at the same time the white man is asking the black man to do this. So all I'm saying is, I absolutely believe the situation can be changed. But I don't think it can be changed by white people taking a hypocritical approach, pretending that it is not as bad as it is, and by black leaders, so-called responsible leaders, taking a hypocritical approach, trying to make white people think that black people are patient

and long-suffering and are willing to sit around
here a long time, or a great deal of time longer,
until the problem is made better.

BERNARD: Let's go back to the phone. The WINS
Contact number; Judson 2-6405. This is Contact,
you're on the air.

GIRL (phoning in): Hello, Malcolm?

MALCOLM: Yes?

GIRL: The Ku Klux Klan should get you.

MALCOLM: Ha-ha-ha-ha—

BERNARD: Thank you very much.

Malcolm was clearly talking revolution but he
would not advocate it. He refused to "tell it like it
is," the only thing the young black militants welcome. Only Allah knows what Malcolm's final fears
were; perhaps the possibility of being charged with
sedition deterred him. Whatever the reason Malcolm forewent' an excellent opportunity to flatly
state that what is needed in this country is a
revolution. Had Malcolm said it, and had luck been
with him, the federal government would have arrested him. Alas, that sequence of events would
have catapulted him into the black leadership position for which he had hungered for so long. But
Malcolm continued to seek some kind of accommodation with the power structure. He was all too
deliberate in his efforts to obey the law and order, a
gesture no revolutionary can afford.

Then there was the phone call, the woman—
obviously white—saying that the KKK should "get"
Malcolm. And the station, despite the mandatory
ten-second-delay button, had allowed the call to be
aired.

Malcolm laughed!

One wonders where—at that moment—was the

Malcolm who had debated me in Chicago? Here is what he said then:

"Who are the real lawbreakers? Any man who brutalizes you when you are attempting to enjoy your constitutional rights...he is the lawbreaker; not you; he is the lawbreaker and he should be treated as one!"

The woman caller had definitely, and publicly, called for Malcolm's death at the hands of white racists. She, not Malcolm, had advocated violence as a solution to problems. The Malcolm I once knew, the de-Muslimized Malcolm the young black militants were seeking, would have then and there promised the woman caller fire in return if not aggressive violence immediately and without further provocation.

Stan Bernard saw the opening and he challenged Malcolm to call for revolution with a taunt; he charged that American black men are too few in number to mount a revolution:

MALCOLM: I say this: The Mau Mau was also a minority, a microscopic minority, but it was the Mau Mau who not only brought independence to Kenya, but—
BERNARD: Within a vast Negro majority.
MALCOLM: But brought it—that wick. The powder keg is always larger than the wick. The smallest thing in the powder keg is the wick. You can touch the powder all day long and nothing happens. It's the wick that you touch that sets the powder off.
BERNARD: I wouldn't want to, I think it'll blow up.
MALCOLM: It's the wick that you touch that sets the powder off. You go here in Harlem, and you take all those moderate Negroes that Dr. Hall here

puts the stamp of approval on, and regards them as responsible—they don't explode. It's the wick, its that small element that you refer to as nationalist and other—

HALL: You're doing all you can to encourage it, Malcolm, with your demagogic language—

MALCOLM: No, no, I don't encourage it; but I'm not going to sit here and pretend that it doesn't exist.

BERNARD: Don't you incite, Malcolm? Don't you incite?

MALCOLM: I don't think so. How are you going to incite people who are living in slums and ghettos? It's the city structure that incites. A city that continues to let people live in rat-nest dens in Harlem and pay higher rent in Harlem than they pay downtown. This is what incites it. Who lets merchants outcharge or overcharge people for their groceries and their clothing and other commodities in Harlem, while you pay less for it downtown. This is what incites it. A city that will not create some kind of employment for people who are barred from having jobs just because their skin is black. That's what incites it. Don't ever accuse a black man for voicing his resentment and dissatisfaction over the criminal condition of his people as being responsible for inciting the situation. You have to indict the society that allows these things to exist. And this is where I differ with Dr. Hall.

BERNARD: Well, in a sense—

HALL: We differ in many places, Malcolm.

MALCOLM: This is another one of the many places where we differ, Dr. Hall.

BERNARD: Well, in a sense, didn't Hitler also talk about different points of view, didn't he say that conditions existed, and didn't he also incite?

MALCOLM: I don't know anything about Hitler, I. wasn't in Germany. I'm in America.

BERNARD: Don't—don't please, Malcolm—

MALCOLM: I say, I wasn't in Germany.

BERNARD: You know about Hitler as well as—

MALCOLM: You can't point to Hitler and Germany behind what's going on here in America! Turn on the television tonight and see what's—

BERNARD: In Harlem—

MALCOLM: No, no, no—turn on the television tonight and see what they're doing to Dr. King.

HALL: Dr. King's methods are not your methods. You couldn't do in Alabama what he is doing.

MALCOLM: Sir—sir—

HALL: You could not do—

MALCOLM: Sir, you had better pray that I don't do and try to do what he is doing. Any time Dr. King—

HALL: Oh, these are just—these are just words, Malcolm—

MALCOLM: Any time Dr. King goes along with people like you—like you—you should put forth more effort to keep him out of jail. You should put forth more effort to protect him. And you should put forth more effort to protect the people who go along with him and display this love and this patience. If you would do more for those people and spend some of your time trying to help these people instead of trying to attack me, probably this country would be a much better place to live. You spend too much of your time, doctor, trying to investigate—

HALL: I rarely ever mention you, Malcolm, you're hardly worth mentioning—

MALCOLM: You spend too much of your time, doctor, running around trying to keep track of dissatisfied black people whom you label as extremists—

HALL: Hardly, hardly—

MALCOLM: —whereas if you would spend some of your time in these places where Dr. King is fighting, then you would make this country a better place to live in.

HALL: Malcolm, I lectured all over the state of Alabama, when you had nothing to do with the Muslims or anybody else.

MALCOLM: Did you have on a white sheet? Did you have on a white sheet?

HALL: See what I mean?

BERNARD: Gentlemen, time. Bell—here we go—bell. O.K. that's round 15. We've just had it.

MALCOLM: Dr. Hall, come up to the Audubon Sunday at two o'clock, and we'll continue from there.

HALL: I have more important things to do.

Malcolm did not realize it but he had finally outwitted the glib Mr. Hall. Indeed Hall should have agreed to attend the Audubon meeting the following Sunday. Hall would have had a front-row seat as the drama of the assassination unfolded.

On Friday Malcolm granted a long—his final—interview to Gordon Parks of *Life* magazine. Parks was later to write.

"(Malcolm) appeared calm and somewhat resplendent with his goatee and astrakhan hat. Much of the old hostility and bitterness seemed to have left him, but the fire and confidence were still there."

Then Malcolm went on to recall his days as a Black Muslim:

"That was a bad scene, brother. The sickness and

madness of those days . . . I am glad to be rid of them. It's time for martyrs now. And if I am to be one, it will be in the cause of brotherhood. That is the only thing that can save this country. I've learned it the hard way—but I learned it.

". . . In many parts of Africa I saw white students helping black people. Something like this kills a lot of arguments. I did many things as a Black Muslim that I'm sorry for now. I was a zombie then—like all Muslims—I was hypnotized, pointed in a certain direction and told to march. Well, I guess a man's entitled to make a fool of himself if he is ready to pay the cost. It cost me twelve years."

Then Gordon Parks put his final question:

"Is it true that killers are stalking you?"

"It is as true as we are standing here," Malcolm X replied. "They have tried it twice in the last two weeks."

"Have you sought police protection?" Parks asked.

"Brother Parks," Malcolm lectured, "nobody can protect you from a Muslim but a Muslim—or someone trained in Muslim tactics. I know; I invented many of those tactics."

On Friday night—tired but driven, confused but obsessed—Malcolm journeyed to Columbia University for what was to be his last public speech. It was a fitting and moving finale for so weary a traveler as Malcolm X. A capacity audience of students and faculty—mostly white—jammed Barnard Gymnasium to hear Malcolm. The Columbia student newspaper later published these excerpts from Malcolm's talk:

We are living in an era of revolution, and the revolt of the American Negro is part of the rebel-

lion against the oppression and colonialism which has characterized his era.

It is incorrect to classify the revolt of the Negro as simply a racial conflict of black against white, or as a purely American problem. Rather, we are today seeing a global rebellion of the oppressed against the oppressor, the exploited against the exploiter.

The Negro revolution is not racial revolt. We are interested in practicing brotherhood with anyone really interested in living according to it. But the white man has long preached an empty doctrine of brotherhood which means little more than a passive acceptance of his fate by the Negro.

(The Western industrial nations have been) deliberately subjugating the Negro for economic reasons. These international criminals raped the African continent to feed their factories, and are themselves responsible for the low standards of living prevalent throughout Africa.

To the end, then, the twin—yet confusing—themes were there. On the one hand the American black man is a part of the non-white revolt that is sweeping the world; on the other hand only racial brotherhood can save America. No program was outlined, no targets named, no ultimatums issued. The final Malcolm was a man whose revolutionary rhetoric was tempered by the ethics of the corrupt society he sought to depose.

On Saturday morning Malcolm moved even deeper into the framework of the American ethic. Accompanied by the real estate broker Malcolm and Sister Betty contracted to buy a house in an integrated, predominantly Jewish, section of Long Island, New York.

The down payment on the home was three thousand dollars; Malcolm and his wife estimated that their moving expenses would be an additional thousand. At that moment Malcolm had less than one hundred and fifty dollars, the financial gleanings of his years of evangelizing and travels.

Then, according to Alex Haley's moving and brilliant reconstruction of the last twenty-four hours of Malcolm's life, Sister Betty and Malcolm returned to the home of the friends who had sheltered them since the fire bombing. Late into the afternoon Malcolm and his wife talked. Malcolm apologised to Sister Betty for the severe and prolonged strains he had forced upon her. "We'll all be together," Malcolm promised. "I want my family with me. Families shouldn't be separated. I'll never make a long trip without you. We'll get somebody to keep the children. I'll never leave you so long again."

Said Sister Betty later: "I couldn't help but just break out grinning."

Malcolm drove into Manhattan where he was to check into the Hilton hotel for the night. On the way he stopped at a phone booth and called Alex Haley. He told Haley about the plans for the house and urged Haley to seek an additional four thousand dollar advance from the publisher of the autobiography. Haley agreed to pursue the matter through the literary agent involved and to report back to Malcolm on Monday night. Then Malcolm changed the subject; in so doing he set off a controversy that rages until this day:

"You know something, brother," Malcolm commented to Haley, "the more I keep thinking about this thing, the things that have happened lately, I'm not sure it is all the Muslims. I know what they can

do, and what they can't, and they can't do some
of the stuff recently going on. Now, I'm going to
tell you, the more I keep thinking about what happened to me in France, I think I'm going to quit
saying it is the Muslims."

Then, in his final remark to Haley, Malcolm
revealed why persons other than the Black Muslims
would assassinate him:

"You know, I'm glad I've been the first to
establish *official* ties between Afro-Americans and
our blood brothers in Africa. Goodbye."

Malcolm X had barely settled in his twelfth-floor
room in the Hilton hotel before the lobby was literally swarming with Negro men who approached
several bellmen demanding to know the number
of Malcolm's room. By then death threats against
Malcolm were reported in practically every edition
of New York City's newspapers and the bellmen
promptly notified the hotel security officer. The hotel
provided Malcolm with tight security.

Malcolm ate dinner alone that night in the
Hilton's semi-dark Bourbon Room as security guards
posing as hotel guests ate dinner at a nearby table.
Malcolm retired to his room, presumably to sleep.

Then there was the loud and piercing ring of the
telephone. It was eight o'clock Sunday morning.

"Yes?" Malcolm answered in his usual manner.

"Wake up, brother," a male caller advised. And
then the phone went dead.

Malcolm telephoned his wife and countermanded
an explicit order he had issued on Saturday
afternoon:

"Will it be too much trouble to dress the children
and bring them to the meeting this afternoon?"

"Of course it won't," Sister Betty replied.

Four hours later Malcolm checked out of the

hotel and drove alone toward his rendezvous with destiny at the Audubon Ballroom.

Then it was well after two o'clock; the meeting was already a half hour late starting. Dr. Milton Galamison, now a member of the New York City board of education, and other Negro notables who were to share the platform with Malcolm had failed to appear. And Malcolm sat alone in the dressing room of the dance hall surrounded by a few of his assistants.

"I don't want to talk about my personal troubles," Malcolm told his assistants. "I don't want that to be the reason for people to come and hear me."

"I am going to tell the people today," Malcolm continued, "that I was too hasty in accusing the Black Muslims of bombing my home. Things have happened that are bigger than they can do. I know what they can do. Things have gone beyond that."

The hour was now late; clearly the black notables, for whatever reasons, had elected not to be associated with Malcolm that afternoon.

"I felt bad," Malcolm's female secretary was to later say. "I felt it was my fault. I felt so terrible for him. It seemed as if no one cared. I told him 'Oh, don't worry, they are just late; they will be here.'"

It was agreed that Brother Benjamin X, a man who had followed Malcolm out of the Black Muslim movement to become his trusted assistant, would speak for thirty minutes and then introduce Malcolm. The clock moved slowly as Benjamin X spoke, reading for the people the words of the great teacher, Malcolm X. The black notables did not arrive. Then, from their places in the dressing room, Malcolm and his other assistants heard Benjamin say:

"And now, without further introduction or remarks, I present to you one who is willing to put himself on the line for you, a man who would give his life for you; I want you to listen, to understand; one who is a Trojan for the black man . . . Minister Malcolm X."

Malcolm rose slowly from his dressing room chair and moved toward the dressing room door leading to the stage. Then he paused and turned to his female assistant. "You'll have to forgive me for being so gruff with you a few minutes ago," he said. "I'm just about at my wits end."

"Don't speak of it," she replied. "I understand."

"I wonder if anybody *really* understands," Malcolm mused, almost to himself as he walked through the door onto the platform.

The several hundred people applauded as Malcolm X, born Malcolm Little and alias Big Red, approached the lectern and gave the Islamic greeting of peace:

"*As-Alaikum-Salaam.*" "Peace also unto you," the people responded.

The greetings of peace were still reverberating through the hall when a scuffle broke out some eight rows from the platform.

"Get your hands out of my pocket," a male voice shouted as the entire audience focused its attention on the melee.

"Cool it, brothers; cool it," Malcolm pleaded, "Cool it!"

It is doubtful that Malcolm ever knew what happened next for he, too, was looking at the melee. But there are those who did see the final act:

As Malcolm looked at the disturbance slightly to his left, three black men sitting together along the front row rose as one, like a firing squad. Their guns roared as indescribable bedlam and terror engulfed the ballroom.

A half hour later a doctor at Columbia-Presbyterian Hospital walked into the emergency receiving room to face crying men and women, including Sister Betty. His announcement was terse:

"The gentleman you know as Malcolm X is dead."

It was then twelve-thirty in Los Angeles. I was preparing for the debate of my television program which was to take place in nine hours. Just that morning I had instructed my producer, Bill Walker, to track down Malcolm X and arrange for him to be a guest on the program at the earliest possible date.

Then came the news bulletin: "Malcolm X, preacher of the anti-white Black Muslim gospel, has been assassinated while addressing a predominantly Negro audience in New York's Harlem. Stay tuned for further details as they come into our newsroom."

After several hours I succeeded in reaching Sister Betty by telephone.

"The niggers *did it*, Lomax," she said. "The niggers *did it!* I didn't believe they would; but the niggers *did it*."

SEVENTEEN

TO KILL A BLACK MAN

The men who assassinated Malcolm X were captured, tried and convicted. They are now serving sentences in the New York State Prison. The man who allegedly assassinated Martin Luther King is awaiting trial in a Memphis jail at this writing. Malcolm's murderers were black men, former members of the Black Muslim movement; Martin's alleged assailant is a nondescript ex-convict and drifter. The easy way out for America is to say that the doers of the deeds have been captured, that justice is served. But that is an all too easy a disposition of the matter.

This society, this violent and corrupt American society, this racist American society assassinated both Malcolm X and Martin Luther King, Jr. The men under arrest may have pulled the trigger, but they by no means acted alone; American society was not only in concert with the assassins but there is every evidence that they were all hired killers.

The key to the matter is the question, "Who would want Malcolm and Martin dead. Why?"

In the case of Malcolm X the finger points inevitably and immediately at Elijah Muhammad. After all Malcolm quit the Black Muslim movement and lured some of Elijah's best followers, including one of Muhammad's sons, to follow him. More, Malcolm persisted in hinting that the movement was rife with scandal, that Elijah was a false prophet who had fleeced the people.

And Malcolm was privy to information about the inner workings of the Black Muslim movement, about the handling of its finances, that could have proved embarrassing. There can be no doubt that the Black Muslims tracked Malcolm every hour of his last days on earth. Their knowledge of his movements was little short of uncanny. Somehow they not only knew the exact time Malcolm was scheduled to arrive in Los Angeles but they knew his hotel as well. They were waiting at his hotel in Chicago when Malcolm drove in from the airport. And they fanned out over the lobby of the Hilton hotel in New York within minutes after Malcolm had checked in for his last night's sleep.

One could dismiss the Los Angeles and Chicago incident by saying Malcolm had telegraphed his moves by making contact with people he wished to see in these two cities. But what about the New York Hilton?

It will be recalled that it was Saturday afternoon; Malcolm and Sister Betty had gone house hunting. Then, in midafternoon, Malcolm left his family with close friends in Queens and made his way to the Hilton where he had planned to rest in seclusion until Sunday afternoon. How did the Black Muslims locate him so quickly?

Then, as Malcolm suddenly divined, there was the strange reaction of the French government. After all one finds it difficult to believe that the French would react so strongly against as insignificant a man as Malcolm X. Or was he insignificant? I am convinced—as Malcolm X was—that the Black Muslims simply do not have the power to persuade the French government to ban anyone as an undesirable person. Think what one may of Elijah, the French episode was beyond his powers and abilities. Malcolm X clearly had enemies other than Elijah Muhammad.

Malcolm had succeeded brilliantly in establishing links with dissident Afro-American groups in various countries, including England and France. His difficulties were at home, with the mass blacks and with members of his own organization. It is hardly news to those knowledgeable about American black militants that links run from Harlem to Cuba, from Cuba to Algeria and Ghana, and from these African countries to such Middle European capitals as Prague. Stokely Carmichael has traveled much the same route, and just last spring a score of ghetto black militants turned up in Prague for a meeting with black revolutionaries from other parts of the world.

Malcolm X was rapidly becoming a major threat to American foreign policy. It is no coincidence that Carl Rowan, a Negro and then head of the United States Information Agency, attacked Malcolm with such bitterness. "An exconvict who became a racial fanatic," Rowan said of Malcolm. As Carl well knew, Malcolm was much more than that. He was a man who captured the imagination of the black ghetto masses and may well have been on his way toward realizing the impossible dream of internationalizing the Negro plight.

And what was the real role of Burke Marshall, then head of the Justice Department's Civil Rights Division, in the drama of Malcolm X? In an extraordinary open move Marshall persuaded the administrators of a philanthropic foundation—and organizations that had donated millions to the civil rights cause—to arrange for him to meet with Alex Haley, then Malcolm's biographer. Marshall bluntly asked Haley the source of Malcolm's funds. Why did Marshall concern himself with the troubled Malcolm who was then wandering through Africa? And why did Malcolm react in silence when Haley told him of the encounter with Marshall?

There is little question that Malcolm had become involved in an international intrigue in what he believed to be the best interests of the American black man. I am also convinced that Malcolm was assassinated by hired killers who carried out the will of those who wished to thwart Malcolm's efforts. And I am convinced that the American government, particularly the CIA, was deeply involved in Malcolm's death.

The men selected as Malcolm's assassins were ideal for the bloody task. They were affiliated with Elijah; they had already been indicted for the January, 1965, shooting of Benjamin Brown, a New York City Correction Officer and a Black Muslim defector. And there is yet another mystery about this that leads me to conclude that men very close to Malcolm were part of the death plot against him.

All of the evidence confirms that the assailants arrived early and secured front row seats in the ballroom. Malcolm was still in the dressing room but his aides and bodyguards were on duty patrolling the hall. For example, Stanley Scott, a Negro reporter, was stopped at the door of the ballroom and told he could enter as a black individual but not as a reporter. Yet three men well known to Malcolm and his aides—men who were then under indictment for the attempted murder of a Black Muslim defector—were allowed to enter the hall and obtain front row center seats and then carry out their mission of death. The very appearance of these men at the ballroom would have caused utmost security measures to go into effect had Malcolm's people been on the alert—or loyal!

Fifteen years seems a relatively light sentence for men who carried out the murder of Malcolm X. It took more than a year to bring them to trial and the mystery was deepened in the interim by the strange death of two people closely associated with Malcolm. And the big gossip item in Harlem is the suddenly acquired affluence of two men who were in charge of protecting Malcolm against harm.

The trial of James Earl Ray, the man charged with the murder of Martin Luther King, is yet to take place. Thus it would be improper to disclose information beyond that which has already been made public. This much can be written, however:

The assassination of King was in no way related to an international intrigue. Rather Martin was slain by someone who carried out the will of an extremely well financed and rigidly organized group of Southern white businessmen. This is not to ignore the strong conviction of Dr. Martin Luther King, Sr., Martin's father, that his son's death was related somehow to that of both the Kennedys. He may well be correct; I think he is. For part and parcel of the Southern syndrome is the notion that civil rights at home and communism abroad are related matters. After having spent several weeks investigating the murder of Martin King I know that the evidence will center around New Orleans —the focus of many investigations into the slaying of John F. Kennedy. The evidence will also show that Ray had contacts with certain persons in Los Angeles and that these same persons were investigated in connection with the assassination of President Kennedy.

The questions as to who pulled the triggers and who paid them aside, the lives and deaths of Malcolm and Martin are classic examples of what America does to some of its best sons, how this society conspires to cut down the very brilliant and creative men who could alter the course of history and lead the republic into the American dream.

America is a white Anglo-Saxon, male society; to the degree that one deviates, either by birth or by choice, from this norm he faces unusual difficulty living out his life as he sees fit, he finds it all but impossible to fully express his gifts and talents. And to the degree that one protests against this flaw in the American way of things one is apt to find himself in danger, mortal danger.

Yet dreamers of the dream continue to protest; they persist in exposing themselves to the possibility that an assassin's bullet will seek to end their crusade. And because of them society moves forward somewhat. As bad as things now are, it cannot be denied that they are better than they once were, that they are somewhat better because Malcolm and Martin were once with us.

Now, then, is the time for martyrdom. And the Black Power people have made of Malcolm a martyr. He is called "Saint Malcolm" and his speeches are read along with those of Che Guevara and the thoughts of Chairman Mao. But those who now make a martyr of Malcolm were not at his side in death; they consistently prostituted his thoughts; they consistently elect not to remember the change toward racial brotherhood that characterized the last weeks of his life. The irony of Malcolm was that he embraced the notion of love at a time in history when it became fashionable for black men to openly express their hate.

For all of his bold talk and searing attacks on the white man, Malcolm never did take to the streets. Rather he warned of the violence brewing in the ghetto; he seemed genuinely interested in curbing it. And at a time when his only hope of realizing full power lay in issuing the bold call for out and out revolution Malcolm began to articulate the ethic of brotherhood.

As for Martin the path toward martyrdom is already dotted with scores of public buildings and parks renamed in his honor. And occasionally one hears a civil rights spokesman—particularly his successor Ralph Abernathy and his widow Coretta King—meekly reissue the call for nonviolence. So immediate and tangible were the social changes Martin engendered while he was alive it is all but impossible to determine just how history will judge him. Unlike other martyrs whose words and deeds influenced change long after they were dead, Martin was an immediate man; he lived to enjoy the fruit of his labor; he lived beyond the days of his successes to the point that people had begun to think of him only in terms of his failures.

. To the end, Martin preached in terms of taming the savage beast in man; he believed black Americans could remain nonviolent and that white power would respond by total sharing. This, of course was not to be the way of ultimate change in America.

And so the formula, the recipe, for killing black men emerges:

Imbue them with the American dream; then deny them the fulfillment of that dream. Tantalize them with the faith that things can be changed through application of the Christian gospel; fill them with guilt if they deviate from this gospel and then violently refuse to respond to their attempts at nonviolent protest. Finally, push the black man to the point where he must violate his own ethical code in order to achieve that which he deems to be good, worthy, and just.

Stir all this well; administer liberal doses in church, in school, at work, in all of the public media, in every aspect of the black man's daily life. Repeat as often as needed.

Death—as Malcolm X and Martin Luther King, Jr. proved—will follow.

Epilogue

Talmadge Hayer, Norman Butler and Thomas Johnson were found guilty of murder in the first degree in the assassination of Malcolm X. James Earl Ray is serving a 99 year sentence in Brushy Mountain Penitentiary in Petros, Tennessee. Lomax was incorrect in his prediction that the investigations of Dr. King's murder would "center around New Orleans" but there is some evidence that James Earl Ray did have contact "with certain persons in Los Angeles." For a fuller account of James Earl Ray and the murder of Dr. King, read The King Conspiracy *by Michael Newton (Holloway House, 1987).*